Michael Bradley's *The Last Words* is a compelling accomplishment in the endless task of saving our history from academic "cultural cleansing."

Those "Last Words" are the catalyst for a deeply reasoned and truly eloquent attack by Mr. Bradley on the practice of "Presentism" by the politicized crusaders of radical academia and their bedfellows in the "mainstream" media.

Any sane American knows at this point that we are "up against it." As always, there are no better weapons in this struggle than the clear, hard facts of history as it actually happened. This precise and wise book from Dr. Bradley and Charleston Athenaeum Press may be one of our generation's most timely calls to action.

—— **Ben Jones** is an actor, author, playwright, comedian, musician, and former United States Congressman from Georgia. He played the beloved "Cooter" in *The Dukes of Hazzard*.

Michael Bradley's book, *The Last Words*, is an important contribution to understanding the truth concerning the North's War to Prevent Confederate Independence. As Gene Kizer states in the Prologue, it is important to understand the viewpoints of those who were living at the time and who experienced the events. Anything else is "Presentism," or history twisted to conform to the politics of today. This collection of Farewell Addresses from men both North and South, will shed much light on the Truth, and dispel the Myth of American History concerning that tragic time.

—— **H. V. Traywick, Jr.** graduated from VMI

in 1967. He is author of *Starlight on the Rails: A Vietnam Veteran's Long Road Home, Empire of the Owls, Virginia Iliad,* and several other books. He received a Bronze Star for his service in Vietnam in the United States Army.

The United States' (previously!) most-revered academic institutions are leading a cultural insurrection whose goal is to completely overthrow the longstanding narrative of American history. Harvard, Yale, Princeton, for example, and even the U.S. Military Academy at West Point are working diligently to promote that single-minded goal. That sad fact is exactly why Michael Bradley's latest book, *The Last Words* (including Gene Kizer, Jr.'s brilliant Prologue, *Setting the Stage*), is so important. Bradley's seventeen "farewell" addresses by Confederate and Union commanders to their troops — their words reflecting their soldiers' service, sacrifice, motives and beliefs, spoken at the end of America's bloodiest war — represent a vitally important window into the past, a great start in exposing the lies and false assumptions promoted by today's academically-brainwashed legions of "identity politics." The only counter-weapon to the militant Left's unrelenting culture-destroying attack on our history is to continue to research, write and publish books like Michael Bradley's *The Last Words.*

—— **Jerry D. Morelock,** PhD
Colonel, U.S. Army, ret.
Senior Historian/Senior Editor,
Historynet.com

Dr. Michael R. Bradley has collected the farewell addresses of both Confederate and Union commanders to their troops, and has also provided a brief biographical sketch of each of these officers, who include Robert E. Lee, Ulysses S. Grant, John S. Mosby, Joseph Wheeler, Nathan Bedford Forrest, and William T. Sherman. Among the biographies of some lesser known officers, one of the most interesting is that of Lt. Colonel Charles T. Trowbridge, a commander of U.S. Colored Troops. I have read Trowbridge's reminiscences, but Dr. Bradley has unearthed much more about him (and about the USCT) that readers will find very revealing. Having researched General Sherman's "march" through Georgia and South Carolina, I find it extremely ironic that in his farewell address to his men he refers to them as "good soldiers." Southern civilians who encountered these troops found most to be quite the opposite. Dr. Bradley's book is not just a collection of historic speeches but also an exploration of what the North and the South were truly fighting for.

—— **Karen Stokes** is an archivist at the S.C. Historical Society and author of ten nonfiction books including *South Carolina Civilians in Sherman's Path* and *A Legion of Devils: Sherman in South Carolina.* Her works of historical fiction include *Honor in the Dust* and *The Immortals.*

Dr. Michael Bradley continues publishing incredibly well-researched, logical and clearly presented works that add immeasurably to our understanding of the war. *The Last Words* is a superlative melding of the farewell addresses by commanders on both sides. With flawless analyses, Dr. Bradley proves why the soldiers fought, using their own words. He contradicts years of politically correct rationales foisted on us by those whose understanding is governed solely by Presentism. This is irrefutable evidence by the soldiers who served in the armies of both sides...a tremendous work.

—— **Lt. Col. (ret) Edwin L. Kennedy, Jr.**
Former Assistant Professor
US Army Command and General Staff College
Fort Leavenworth, KS

Noted historian of the War Between the States, Dr. Michael Bradley, has written an important volume that will be of great value to both researchers and readers interested in how that conflict ended, what its various commanders wished to communicate to their troops, and what their words mean for posterity.

Dr. Bradley puts things into historical context and assists us in seeing first-hand what was occurring. In so doing we are given a deep insight into our history and our memory.

Editor Gene Kizer Jr. has done an excellent job in preparing this edition, and he contributes an outstanding forty-seven page Prologue, *Setting the Stage.* A full bibliography, numerous and detailed footnotes, and a full index add to this volume's value.

—— **Dr. Boyd Cathey** has served as State Registrar of the North Carolina Division of Archives and History. He has published in French, Spanish, and English, on historical subjects as well as classical music and opera.

A few of the books by
Michael R. Bradley

Tullahoma: The 1863 Campaign for the Control of Middle Tennessee

With Blood and Fire: Life Behind Union Lines in Middle Tennessee, 1863-65

Nathan Bedford Forrest's Escort & Staff in War and Peace

They Rode with Forrest

It Happened in the Revolutionary War: Stories of Events and People that Shaped American History

It Happened in the Civil War

Forrest's Fighting Preacher: David Campbell Kelley of Tennessee

Murfreesboro in the Civil War (co-author)

The Raiding Winter

Civil War Myths and Legends: The True Stories Behind History's Mysteries

Death in the Great Smoky Mountains

The Last Words

Charleston Athenaeum Press

The Last Words

The Farewell Addresses

of

Union and Confederate Commanders

to Their Men at the End of the

War Between the States

Michael R. Bradley

Charleston Athenaeum Press
Charleston, South Carolina

Charleston Athenaeum Press

Post Office Box 13012
Charleston, SC 29422-3012

Please order books from
www.CharlestonAthenaeumPress.com

ISBN: 978-0-9853632-4-6 *Softcover*
Library of Congress Control Number: 2022939960
ISBN: 978-0-9853632-5-3 *Hardback*
ISBN: 978-0-9853632-8-4 *Ebook*

Publisher's Cataloging-in-Publication Data

Names: Bradley, Michael R. (Michael Raymond), 1940-, author.
Title: The last words : the farewell addresses of Union and Confederate commanders to their men at the end of the war between the states / Michael R. Bradley.
Description: Includes bibliographical references and index. | Charleston, SC: Charleston Athenaeum Press, 2022.
Identifiers: LCCN: 2022939960 | ISBN 978-0-9853632-5-3 (hardcover) | 978-0-9853632-4-6 (paperback) | 978-0-9853632-8-4 (ebook)
Subjects: LCSH United States–History–Civil War, 1861-1865. | Speeches, addresses, etc., American. | United States–History–Civil War, 1861-1865–Sources. | BISAC HISTORY / United States / Civil War Period (1850-1877)
Classification: LCC E464 .B73 2022 | DDC 973.3–dc23

First Print Edition
July, 2022

This book is dedicated to

Pvt. John Calhoun Bradley,
11th Tennessee Cavalry

Pvt. Andrew Jackson Bradley,
1st Tennessee Infantry

Sgt. John Newton Todd,
Orr's South Carolina Rifles

Pvt. Elias F. Alexander,
1st South Carolina Cavalry

and all the others like them who spoke from
their hearts about their love of family and home.
We who are descended from them have not
forgotten them.

Acknowledgments

Thanks are due many people in the production of any book. Gene Kizer has worked long and patiently with me in bringing this work from a concept to a finished product. My wife has tolerated my eccentricities as I engaged in research in archives and on-line in tracking down the material used in writing. Many friends who have read other of my books have been supportive in encouraging me to "stay the course" in working on *The Last Words*.

Mrs. Susan Harris planted the idea for the book in my mind. We were on adjacent treadmills at the gym one day when she asked "Is there a book about what officers said to their men when the war was over?" I replied, "No, but there will be." Inspiration strikes in the most unusual places.

Contents

"Never mind that anyone touring a battlefield cannot find a single monument to Union soldiers which boasts that the men fought to end slavery. They all honor the bravery of those who fought and died, and speak of preserving the Union. Perhaps this emphasis on preserving the Union is why historians almost always call the United States forces the "Union Army" despite the fact that this name displaces slavery as the central factor supposedly causing the war."

From the *Introduction*,
by the Author

Prologue

Setting the Stage

To understand the past you have to look at the past the way the people who lived in the past looked at it. It was the present to them just as today is our unfortunate present. So-called historians and journalists judging the past by the goofy standards of today falsify history and feed us political propaganda. They aren't seeking truth. Read the words of the people of the past, study the conditions of their lives and make up your own mind.

by Gene Kizer, Jr.,
Charleston Athenaeum Press

𝕷ieutenant T. J. Cureton of Company B, the Waxhaw Jackson Guards, fought all three days at the Battle of Gettysburg in the famous Twenty-sixth North Carolina Regiment. They were nearly wiped out the first day and survivors were in Pickett's Charge two days later on July 3, 1863.

Cureton describes the charge that third day in a letter after the war stating that Union artillery opened on them "a half mile of the works" but Confederate lines "crossed the lane in splendid order when about two hundred yards from their works the musketry opened on us."[1]

By the time those North Carolina boys got to within forty yards through booming cannons, smoke and murderous fire with dead and mangled bodies all around "our regiment had been reduced to a skirmish line" but still kept "closing to the colours."[2]

Through the confusion he heard a cry from Davis's Mississippi Brigade to the left and turned to see it wiped off the face of the earth by artillery fire like "chaff before a 'whirl wind'"[3]

He sums it up:

> [T]he gallant old 26th Regiment had sixty-seven muskets and three officers present on the night July 3

[1] Letter from T. J. Cureton to Colonel J. R. Lane, 22 June 1890, Lane Papers, in Archie K. Davis, *Boy Colonel of the Confederacy, The Life and Times of Henry King Burgwyn, Jr.* (Chapel Hill: The University of North Carolina Press, 1985), Appendix, 351.
[2] Ibid.
[3] Ibid.

1863 of the eight hundred and fifty carried in the fight July 1st 1863.[4]

Death 'reigned with universal sway' in the War Between the States.[5]

In the book *This Republic of Suffering, Death and the American Civil War,* historian Drew Gilpin Faust writes:

> In the middle of the nineteenth century, the United States embarked on a new relationship with death, entering into a civil war that proved bloodier than any other conflict in American history, a war that would presage the slaughter of World War I's Western Front and the global carnage of the twentieth century.[6]

Dead soldiers in the War Between the

---

[4] Ibid. The Twenty-sixth North Carolina Regiment covered itself in glory at Gettysburg. William F. Fox, in *Regimental Losses in the American Civil War*, states that it suffered "the severest regimental loss during the war."
[5] Drew Gilpin Faust, *This Republic of Suffering, Death and the American Civil War* (New York: Alfred A. Knopf, 2008), xiii. The statement was made by a Confederate soldier.
[6] Faust, *This Republic of Suffering*, xi.

States

> were equal to the total American
> fatalities in the Revolution, the
> War of 1812, the Mexican War, the
> Spanish-American War, World
> War I, World War II, and the
> Korean War combined.[7]

Faust writes that 620,000 died. Those are the long-accepted figures of Union officer William F. Fox who, in the 1890s, counted losses regiment by regiment.[8]

Fox knew his numbers were low because of incomplete records from the devastated South and other problems with undercounting.

Fox's numbers were updated in 2011 by historian J. David Hacker who analyzed census records for three decades, the decades before, during and after the war, using techniques such as comparing female survival rates with male, to come up with a range of 650,000 to 850,000 deaths. The midpoint, 750,000, has become widely accepted. James McPherson calls that number "plausible."[9]

---

[7] Ibid.

[8] William F. Fox, *Regimental Losses in the American Civil War* (Albany, N.Y.: Joseph McDonough, 1898).

[9] Rachel Coker, "Historian revises estimate of Civil War dead," published September 21, 2011, Binghamton University Research News - Insights and Innovations

That number is more horrifying when one considers that there were only 31.4 million people in the country when the war started.[10]

Compare the 750,000 dead of the War Between the States with the 419,400 dead of World War II out of a national population of 132,164,569.

Consider the carnage. Faust quotes historian James McPherson:

> [T]he overall mortality rate for the South exceeded that of any country in World War I and that of all but the region between the Rhine and the Volga in World War II.[11]

---

from Binghamton University, http://discovere.binghamton.edu/news/civilwar-3826.html, accessed July 7, 2014. See also Bob Zeller, "How Many Died in the American Civil War?", January 6, 2022, https://www.history.com/news/american-civil-war-deaths, accessed 3-8-22; and Jennie Cohen, "Civil War Deadlier Than Previously Thought?", https://www.history.com/news/civil-war-deadlier-than-previously-thought, accessed 3-8-22.

[10] The United States Census Bureau on their website lists 31,443,321 as the population of the United States in 1860 according to the "Eighth Census under the Secretary of the Interior." https://www.census.gov/history/www/through_the_deades/fast_facts/1860_fast_facts.html, accessed 3-7-22.

[11] Faust, *This Republic of Suffering*, xii. She cites James

Historian Phil Leigh writes:

> At least five percent of the white population of the eleven Confederate states, from which the government drew her soldiers, were killed during the Civil War. If America were to go to war presently and suffer the same death ratio [as the South], the number of killed would total seventeen million. That is more than forty times the number of American deaths during World War II.[12]

Leigh is making the point that:

> Given the magnitude of such losses, nobody with common sense could believe that the prime motive to erect and display memorials to seventeen million

M. McPherson, *Crossroads of Freedom: Antietam* (New York: Oxford University Press, 2002) pp. 3, 177, n. 56.
[12] Phil Leigh, "Ketanji Jackson and the Confederate Flag," Civil War Chat, https://civilwarchat.wordpress.com/2022/03/21/ketanji-jackson-and-the-confederate-flag, accessed 3-22-22.

dead . . . would be anything other
than to honor their memory.[13]

The War Between the States was not only
bloody, it changed our government forever. It is
commonly referred to as the central event in
American history.

We went from the republic of the Founding
Fathers in which states were supreme and sovereign,[14] to a consolidated national government
that was supreme over the states.

Southerners had wanted their states supreme and sovereign forever: States' Rights. The
Preamble to the Confederate Constitution

---

[13] Ibid.

[14] The Treaty of Paris at the end of the Revolutionary
War stated in Article 1: "His Britannic Majesty acknowl-
edges the said United States, viz: New Hampshire,
Massachusetts Bay, Rhode Island and Providence
Plantations, Connecticut, New York, New Jersey, Penn-
sylvania, Delaware, Maryland, Virginia, North Carolina,
South Carolina and Georgia, to be FREE, SOVEREIGN
AND INDEPENDENT STATES; that he treats with them
as such; and for himself his heirs and successors, re-
linquishes all claims to the government, propriety and
territorial rights of the same and every part thereof."
(Emphasis used by Christopher Memminger in the
"Declaration of the Immediate Causes Which Induce and
Justify the Secession of South Carolina from the Federal
Union," adopted December 24, 1860 in S.C.'s secession
convention, from where this quotation was taken.).

makes that clear:

> We, the people of the Confederate
> States, each State acting in its
> **sovereign** and independent
> character, in order to form a
> permanent federal government,
> establish justice, insure domestic
> tranquillity, and secure the
> blessings of liberty to ourselves
> and our posterity invoking the
> favor and guidance of Almighty
> God do ordain and establish this
> Constitution for the Confederate
> States of America. (Bold emphasis
> added)

But Northerners wanted the federal government supreme. They were the "Federals" in the war.

They wanted to control the country's economy, banking, money, commerce, taxes, tariffs and wealth by controlling the federal government.

Federal legislation giving Northerners monopolies, bounties and subsidies for their businesses that were always paid out of the national treasury had made them rich and powerful.

Georgia's declaration of causes for its secession had accurately stated:

> The material prosperity of the
> North was greatly dependent on
> the Federal Government; that of
> the South not at all.[15]

Yet, Southerners were producing the wealth of the country with their agriculture. Southern agricultural commodities "accounted for close to 82% of [the] U.S. export business"[16] in a global plantation economy. Cotton alone was over 60% of U.S. exports in 1860.

And Southerners were paying 83% of the country's taxes while 80% of the tax money was being spent in the North.[17]

To show what was truly at stake in the country just before the war, contrast these Northern and Southern statements within three weeks of

---

[15] *Report on the Causes of the Secession of Georgia* adopted by the Georgia Secession Convention, Tuesday, 29 January 1861, in the *Journal of the Georgia Convention*, in *The War of the Rebellion: A Compilation of the Official Records of the Union and Confederate Armies* (Washington: Government Printing Office, 1900); reprint, Historical Times Inc., 1985, Series IV, Volume 1.

[16] Samuel W. Mitcham, Jr., *It Wasn't About Slavery, Exposing the Great Lie of the Civil War* (Washington, DC: Regnery History, 2020), 114.

[17] Ibid.

each other starting with Georgia Senator Robert Toombs who gives us a perfect analogy — the North as a suction pump sucking money out of the South — via

> bounties and protection to every interest and every pursuit in the North, to the extent of at least fifty millions per annum, besides the expenditure of at least sixty millions out of every seventy of the public expenditure among them, thus making the treasury a perpetual fertilizing stream to them and their industry, and a suction-pump to drain away our substance and parch up our lands.[18]

Here is *The Daily Chicago Times* in abject panic December 10, 1860, a week before South Carolina's secession convention was to convene:

> In one single blow our foreign

---

[18] Robert Toombs, "Secessionist Speech, Tuesday Evening, November 13" delivered to the Georgia legislature in Milledgeville November 13, 1860, in William W. Freehling and Craig M. Simpson *Secession Debated, Georgia's Showdown in 1860* (New York: Oxford University Press, 1992), 38.

commerce must be reduced to less than one-half what it now is. Our coastwise trade would pass into other hands. One-half of our shipping would lie idle at our wharves. We should lose our trade with the South, with all its **immense profits.** Our manufactories would be in utter ruins. Let the South adopt the free-trade system, or that of a tariff for revenue, and these results would likely follow. If protection be wholly withdrawn from our labor, it could not complete, with all the prejudices against it, with the labor of Europe. We should be driven from the market, and millions of our people would be compelled to go out of employment. (Bold emphasis added)[19]

The title of the editorial above is "The Value of the Union," which shows why the Union was

---

[19] *Daily Chicago Times*, "The Value of the Union," December 10, 1860, in Howard Cecil Perkins, ed., *Northern Editorials on Secession*, Vol II (Gloucester: Peter Smith, 1964), 573-574.

the lifeblood of the North. It had given them all their wealth and power. Without it their economy was dead.

That is why Abraham Lincoln said over and over and over that the war was being fought for the preservation of the Union, not to end slavery.

Lincoln wrote Horace Greeley August 22, 1862, sixteen months into the war, and again made that clear. The italics are Lincoln's:

> . . . My paramount object in this struggle *is* to save the Union, and is *not* either to save or to destroy slavery. If I could save the Union without freeing *any* slave I would do it, and if I could save it by freeing *all* the slaves I would do it; and if I could save it by freeing some and leaving others alone I would also do that—What I do about slavery, and the colored race, I do because I believe it helps to save the Union; and what I forbear, I forbear because I do *not* believe it would help the Union.[20]

---

[20] Letter, A. Lincoln to Horace Greeley, August 22, 1862, in Roy P. Basler, ed., *The Collected Works of Abraham Lincoln* (New Brunswick, NJ: Rutgers University Press,

To Southerners, the Union had become a violent, lawless threat to their safety. Northerners financed John Brown and sent him and his murderers into the peaceful communities of the South to rape, destroy and kill then hailed him as a hero when brought to justice.

The Republican Party printed Hinton Helper's *The Impending Crisis of the South* as a campaign document, which called for the throats of Southerners to be cut in the night. Republicans printed hundreds of thousands of copies and distributed them coast to coast.

George Washington warned that sectional political parties would destroy the country but Wendell Phillips proudly stated that the Republican Party

> is the first sectional party ever
> organized in this country. It does
> not know its own face, and calls
> itself national; but it is not
> national—it is sectional. The
> Republican Party is a party of the
> North pledged against the South.[21]

1953) V:388.

[21] Wendell Phillips quotation in Albert Taylor Bledsoe *Is Davis A Traitor; or Was Secession a Constitutional Right Previous to The War of 1861?* (Baltimore: Innes & Company, 1866); reprint, (North Charleston, SC: Fletcher and Fletcher Publishing, 1995), 250. Lincoln, whom over 60%

Northerners began realizing how critical the Union was to their well being. Editorials like "The Value of the Union" began appearing all over the North. New York City threatened to secede from New York State over its enormous trade with the South.

Horace Greeley acknowledged the right of secession and self-government in a long emotional editorial entitled "The Right of Secession"[22] in which he quoted the Declaration of Independence stating "governments 'derive their just powers from the consent of the governed; and that, whenever any form of government becomes destructive of these ends, it is the right of the people to alter or abolish it, and institute a new government."

That was the most widely quoted phrase in the South in the secession debate that took place in the year prior to states seceding.

Greeley went on: "We do heartily accept this doctrine, believing it intrinsically sound, benefi-

---

of the country voted against, "was the first and only sectional president in American history." See Donald W. Livingston, "The Secession Tradition in America" in David Gordon, ed., *Secession, State & Liberty* (New Brunswick NJ: Transaction Publishers, 2002), 27.

[22] "The Right of Secession," The *New-York Daily Tribune,* December 17, 1860, in Howard Cecil Perkins, ed., *Northern Editorials on Secession* (Gloucester, MA: Peter Smith, 1964), 199-201.

cent, and one that, universally accepted, is calculated to prevent the shedding of seas of human blood" and

> if it justified the secession from
> the British Empire of Three
> Millions of colonists in 1776, we
> do not see why it would not justify
> the secession of Five Millions of
> Southrons from the Federal Union
> in 1861.

Greeley says "we could not stand up for coercion, for subjugation, for we do not think it would be just. We hold the right of Self-Government sacred" and we should "Let Them Go!" but when this sniveling hypocrite realized Southern secession would affect his money, he wanted war like the rest of the North.

Northerners were pouring drool like a pack of starving wolves before tearing a lamb to bits to win the election of 1860, control the Federal Government and rule the country with their larger population.[23]

---

[23] Alexis de Tocqueville predicted in *Democracy in America* that if any one state got control of the federal government it would make the rest of the country tributary to its wealth and power and that is exactly what happened except it wasn't one state but all the close-knit Northern states with their commercial-industrial interests.

That is exactly the "tyranny of the majority" the Founding Fathers warned about, but as South Carolina stated:

> [W]hen vast sectional interests are
> to be subserved, involving the
> appropriation of countless millions
> of money, it has not been the usual
> experience of mankind, that words
> on parchments can arrest power.[24]

So many of the politicized "historians" in academia and the idiot news media today proclaim that slavery was the cause of the war but one can prove beyond the shadow of a doubt that the North did not go to war to end slavery.

All Northern documents before and up to two years into the war — after hundreds of thousands of men had been killed — strongly supported slavery.

Six slave states, or 25% of Union states, fought for the North the entire war.[25] That,

---

[24] "Address of the People of South Carolina, Assembled in Convention, to the People of the Slaveholding States of the United States," adopted 24 December 1860 by the South Carolina Secession Convention, Charleston, S.C., in John Amasa May and Joan Reynolds Faunt, *South Carolina Secedes* (Columbia: University of South Carolina Press, 1960), 82-92.

[25] The Union slave states were Maryland, Delaware,

alone, proves the war was not fought over slavery.

If the North was fighting a war to end slavery, they would have first ended it in their own country by passing a constitutional amendment abolishing slavery.

Instead, they passed the Corwin Amendment, which would have left black people in slavery forever even beyond the reach of Congress in places where slavery already existed.

Lincoln strongly supported the Corwin Amendment and lobbied the governors to pass it in their states. He said in his first inaugural, "holding such a provision to now be implied constitutional law, I have no objection to its being made express and irrevocable." Five Union states ratified the Corwin Amendment before the war made it moot.[26]

The Northern War Aims Resolution passed in July, 1861, three months into the war stated:

Missouri, Kentucky, New Jersey, and West Virginia, which came into the Union as a slave state just weeks *after* the Emancipation Proclamation went into effect. The Emancipation Proclamation exempted all six Union slave states as well as Confederate territory already under Union control.

[26] Union states ratifying the Corwin Amendment are "Kentucky, Ohio, Rhode Island, Maryland, and Illinois." See Samuel W. Mitcham, Jr. *It Wasn't About Slavery, Exposing the Great Lie of the Civil War* (Washington, DC: Regnery History, 2020), 127.

> ... That this war is not waged
> upon our part in any spirit of
> oppression, nor for any purpose of
> conquest or subjugation, **nor for
> the purpose of overthrowing or
> interfering with the rights or
> institutions [slavery] of the
> States, but to defend and
> maintain the supremacy of the
> Constitution** [which allowed and
> protected slavery], and to
> **preserve the Union. ...** [27] (Bold
> emphasis added)

Even the Preliminary Emancipation Proclamation issued September 22, 1862, just weeks before the actual Emancipation Proclamation, states in the first paragraph:

> I, Abraham Lincoln, President of
> the United States of America, and

---

[27] The War Aims Resolution is also known by the names of its sponsors, Representative John. J. Crittenden of Kentucky and Senator Andrew Johnson of Tennessee: The Crittenden-Johnson Resolution, or just the Crittenden Resolution. It passed the U.S. House of Representatives July 22, 1861 and the Senate July 25, 1861. There were only two dissenting votes in the House and five in the Senate. http://en.wikipedia.org/wiki/Crittenden-Johnson_Resolution, accessed April 19, 2022.

Commander-in-Chief of the Army
and Navy thereof, do hereby
proclaim and declare that
hereafter, as heretofore, the
war will be prosecuted for the
object of practically restoring the
constitutional relation between the
United States, and each of the
States, and the people thereof, in
which States that relation is, or
may be, suspended or disturbed.
(Bold emphasis added)[28]

There are legion statements by Abraham
Lincoln out there supporting slavery such as this
one in his first inaugural made before he stated
his support for the Corwin Amendment:

I have no purpose, directly or
indirectly, to interfere with the

---

[28] The next paragraph of the Preliminary Emancipation
Proclamation expressed another of Lincoln's beliefs, that
black people should be shipped back to Africa or into a
place they could survive: ". . . the effort to colonize
persons of African descent, with their consent, upon this
continent, or elsewhere, with the previously obtained
consent of the Governments existing there, will be continued." See "Preliminary Emancipation Proclamation,
September 22,1862" at https://www.archives.gov/
exhibits/american_originals_iv/sections/transcript_
preliminary_emancipation.html, accessed 4-12-22.

institution of slavery in the States
where it exists. I believe I have no
lawful right to do so, and I have no
inclination to do so.

The proof is overwhelming and conclusive
that the North did not go to war to free the
slaves.

The North went to war because its economy
was dependent on Southern cotton and without
it they were headed for economic annihilation.

In 1860, the South was "producing 66 percent of the world's cotton, and raw cotton accounted for more than half [over 60% alone] of
all U.S. exports."[29]

The American cotton industry before the
war was awesome to behold. The *New York
Tribune* agriculture editor, Solon Robinson, in
1848, wrote about '"acres of cotton bales"' on the
docks in New Orleans:

Boats are constantly arriving, so
piled up with cotton, that the lower
tier of bales on deck are in the
water; and as the boat is

---

[29] Anne Farrow, Joel Lang, and Jenifer Frank, *Complicity, How the North Promoted, Prolonged, and Profited
from Slavery* (New York: Ballantine Books, Copyright
2005 by The Hartford Courant Company), 7.

approaching, it looks like a huge
raft of cotton bales, with the
chimneys and steam pipe of an
engine sticking up out of the
centre.[30]

King Cotton was "the backbone of the
American economy" and "the North ruled the
kingdom."[31] Southerners grew the cotton and
Northerners did everything else:

> Northern merchants, shippers,
> and financial institutions, many
> based in New York City, were
> crucial players in every phase of
> the national and international
> cotton trade. Meanwhile, the
> rivers and streams of the North,
> particularly in New England, were
> crowded with hundreds of textile
> mills. Well before the Civil War,
> the economy of the entire North
> relied heavily on cotton grown by
> millions of slaves—in the South.[32]

Ralph Waldo Emerson wrote that '"Cotton

---

[30] Ibid.

[31] Ibid.

[32] Farrow, Lang, Frank, *Complicity*, xxvi.

thread holds the union together; unites John C. Calhoun and Abbott Lawrence. Patriotism for holidays and summer evenings, with music and rockets, but cotton thread is the Union.'"[33]

Without the South, the North was in serious economic trouble. Southerners had made protective tariffs unconstitutional. They had a 10% tariff for the operation of a small federal government in a States' Rights nation.

At the same time, economically ignorant Northerners passed the astronomical Morrill Tariff that was 37 to 50% higher. It threatened to reroute the Northern shipping industry into the South overnight because nobody was going to ship into the North and pay a 47 to 60% tariff when they could ship into the South and pay 10%.

The Morrill Tariff meant that Northern ship captains would have a hard time getting cargoes in the North but in the South they would be guaranteed all the cargoes they could handle of cotton and other valuable Southern commodities to transport around the world.

Those same ship captains would then be able to bring cargoes back from around the world and into warm water Southern ports where they would be put on boats in the Mis-

---

sissippi, and on railroads, and shipped to all parts of the Union.

Northerners could have passed a tariff competitive with the South but they didn't.

Because of Northern greed and economic stupidity, the Morrill Tariff threatened to give Southerners a gift of much of the commerce of the entire country.

The Northern manufacturing industry faced obliteration too because over half of its market was its captive market in the South. Independent Southerners would not be buying overpriced goods from people who sent murderers into their country to kill them.

Southerners had for decades wanted free trade with Europe so they could get out from under extortionate Northern prices for inferior goods jacked up by Yankee tariffs and monopolies.

South Carolina almost seceded thirty-three years earlier over the Tariff of Abominations, and should have.

Great Britain was the dominant economic and military power on earth in the 1860s. The cotton gin, short for "cotton engine," had revolutionized cotton production, which had led to an ironclad relationship between the South and Great Britain:

> By the eve of the Civil War,
> Great Britain was largely clothing
> the Western world, using Southern-
> grown, slave-picked cotton.[34]

All Southerners had to do was establish formal trade and military treaties with Great Britain, with whom they already had an "iron-clad" relationship because of cotton, and the North would not be able to beat the South in a war.

Lincoln knew all this and was not going to allow the free-trade Confederate States of America to rise to power on his southern border.

He knew that the future of the American nation for at least the next century, maybe forever, was at stake right then.

That's why, with four times the white population of the South, enormous weapon manufacturing capability, a pipeline to the wretched refuse of the world with which to feed Union armies (25% of the Union army was foreign born), an army, navy and other advantages at that point in history, he sent five hostile military missions into Southern waters in March and April, 1861 to start a war.[35]

---

[34] Farrow, Lang, Frank, *Complicity*, 10. Eli Whitney patented his cotton gin in 1794.

[35] Mitcham, *It Wasn't About Slavery*, 142. Mitcham states

Several Northern newspapers such as the *Providence (R.I.) Daily Post* saw exactly what Lincoln was doing. In an editorial entitled "WHY?" published the day after the commencement of the bombardment of Fort Sumter, April 13, 1861, it wrote:

> We are to have civil war, if at all,
> because Abraham Lincoln loves a
> party better than he loves his
> country. . . . Mr. Lincoln saw an
> opportunity to inaugurate civil war
> without appearing in the character
> of an aggressor.

The *New York Herald* eight days earlier wrote:

> We have no doubt Mr. Lincoln
> wants [President Davis] to take
> the initiative in capturing . . . forts
> in its waters, for it would give him

---

that by the first of April, 1861, the following five military expeditions were "in, steaming toward, or about to sail for Southern territorial waters:

1) the Welles-Fox Expedition, heading for Charleston;
2) the Rowan Expedition, also heading for Charleston;
3) Captain Adams' ships, lurking off Santa Rosa Island;
4) Colonel Brown's Expedition, heading for Pensacola;
5) Porter's Expedition, also steaming for Pensacola."

the opportunity of throwing [to the South] the responsibility of commencing hostilities.[36]

One gets little debate in Woke academia or the idiot news media on the cause of the war because vigorous debate is impossible. Those institutions are virtually 100% liberal and tow the Woke liberal line so the enraged mob doesn't show up at their office or, God forbid, accuse them of being a racist.

Forty years ago, historian Joe Gray Taylor wanted to examine the causes of the war but quickly concluded that esteemed historian David H. Donald was "correct when he said in 1960 that the causation of the Civil War was dead as a serious subject of historical analysis" and that "A 'Southern' point of view on the secession crisis no longer exists among professional historians."[37]

Without a "'Southern' point of view on the secession crisis" you can never get to the truth

---

[36] Editorial, *New York Herald*, April 5, 1861, in Mitcham, *It Wasn't About Slavery*, 147.

[37] Joe Gray Taylor, "The White South from Secession to Redemption," in John B. Boles and Evelyn Thomas Nolen, *Interpreting Southern History, Historiographical Essays in Honor of Sanford W. Higginbotham* (Baton Rouge: Louisiana State University Press, 1987), 162-164.

of American history. You can not have a debate
with only one side presented. The Bible in Prov-
erbs 18:17 says "The first to state his case seems
right until another comes and cross-examines
him."

In the 1960s, academia and the news media
went from truth as their standard, to the political
advantage of the left as their standard, because,
as stated, they are virtually 100% liberal.

Like the political operatives they are, so
much of their history is filthy politics, not truth.
They want to control the past so they can control
the future, like Orwell said:

> Who controls the past controls the
> future: who controls the present
> controls the past.[38]

To have a debate and get at the truth both
sides need to be represented 50/50 so they can
challenge each other to the full extend of their
intelligence, knowledge and passion and see
who has the stronger argument.

Politicized academia and the idiot news
media are 100/0 so truth is impossible yet if you
don't agree with their Woke history, you are a

---

[38] George Orwell, *1984* (New York: New American
Library, 1950), 32. This was one of the slogans of Big
Brother's English Socialist Party of Oceania, INGSOC.

racist hatemonger who deserves to die and certainly not have a career.

Esteemed historian Eugene Genovese (*Roll Jordan Roll, The World the Slaves Made,* et al.) said 30 years ago that to speak positively about the Old South

> is to invite charges of being a racist and an apologist for slavery and segregation. **We are witnessing a cultural and political atrocity** — an increasingly successful campaign by the media and an academic elite to strip young white Southerners, and arguably black Southerners as well, of their heritage . . . [39] (Bold emphasis added)

The destruction of century old historic monuments to Southern war dead is also a cultural and political atrocity, and it is immoral.

Those monuments are gifts from the people of the past to the people of the future. Their

---

[39] Eugene D. Genovese, *The Southern Tradition, The Achievement and Limitations of an American Conservatism* (Cambridge: Harvard University Press, 1994), xi-xii.

destruction denies the people of the future the opportunity to gaze on them and read the inscriptions and ponder for themselves what happened in the past.

Much has been written in the past 40 years on the politicization of our history and its unavoidable result, the falsification of our history. Allan Bloom, in his 1987 book, *The Closing of the American Mind,* confirms that "humanities and social science departments within universities [where History resides] had abandoned objectivity and truth and become hopelessly politicized."[40]

David Harlan, in his book *The Degradation of American History,* explains how it began. He says that, starting in the 1960s with the Civil Rights Movement, leftist historians began criticizing American history as elitist. He writes that academia wanted to expose the complicity of white men "in the violence and brutality that now seemed to be the most important truth about American history." They "feel no need to say what is good in American history."[41]

---

[40] Allan Bloom, *The Closing of the American Mind*, in Keith Windschuttle, *The Killing of History, How Literary Critics and Social Theorists Are Murdering Our Past* (New York: The Free Press, 1996), 10.
[41] David Harlan, *The Degradation of American History* (Chicago: University of Chicago Press, 1997), xv. This paragraph, written by me, comes verbatim from the

Keith Windschuttle, in *The Killing of History,* writes that most young people today are "taught to scorn the traditional values of Western culture - equality, freedom, democracy, human rights - as hollow rhetoric used to mask the self-interest of the wealthy and powerful. This teaching, Bloom argued, had bred a cynical, amoral, self-centered younger generation who lacked any sense of inherited wisdom from the past."

Windschuttle points out that for 2,400 years history has ranked "with philosophy and mathematics as among the most profound and enduring contributions that ancient Greece made, not only to European civilization, but to the human species as a whole." History's "essence" has been to "tell the truth, to describe as best as possible what really happened" but today, in much of academia and the news media, "these assumptions are widely rejected."[42]

Many in the humanities and social sciences "assert that it is impossible to tell the truth about the past" because "we can only see the past through the perspective of our own culture and, hence, what we see in history are our own in-

Introduction to my book, *Charles W. Ramsdell, Dean of Southern Historians, Volume One: His Best Work* (Charleston: Charleston Athenaeum Press, 2017).
[42] Keith Windschuttle, *The Killing of History, How Literary Critics and Social Theorists Are Murdering Our Past* (New York: The Free Press, 1996), 1-2.

terests and concerns reflected back at us."

Because of this, supposedly, the entire point of history is no longer valid therefore "there is no fundamental distinction any more between history and myth" or between "fiction and non-fiction."[43]

In other words, nothing exists except what Woke political liberals in academia and the idiot news media tell us exists.

Academia's hate is having their desired effect. Dr. Edward M. Gilbreth noted in his *Post and Courier* (Charleston, S.C.) column on July 15, 2021 that in the demographic of 18-24 year olds, a recent Issues and Insights poll finds that only "36 percent of them say they are very or extremely proud to be Americans."

In contrast, that same poll finds that "68 percent of adults say they are 'very' or 'extremely' proud to be an American, with another 15 'moderately' proud." The 18-24 demographic was the only one less than 50%.

Dr. Gilbreth concludes that "attempts to describe the country as corrupt, racist, unfair and in need of 'transformation' have not had much impact on the general population" but it has on young people.

Distinguished professor emeritus of History of the University of South Carolina in Columbia,

---

[43] Windschuttle, *The Killing of History*, 2, 7.

Clyde N. Wilson, states:

> [D]espite the thirst for history and
> the centrality of historical thinking
> in our consciousness, academic
> historians have never been more
> irrelevant, incestuous, and
> unreadable.[44]

We are living in Orwell's Oceania, where, as James S. Robbins writes in *Erasing America, Losing Our Future by Destroying Our Past*:

> Progressives seek to demean and
> demolish, elevating the victims of
> the past as an indictment of the
> present. They wield history as a
> weapon on behalf of the
> aggrieved, never gratified by the
> progress made. Indeed, as one
> supposed injustice after another is

---

[44] Clyde Wilson, February 12, 2019 Review of *Historical Consciousness or the Remembered Past* by John Lukacs (Schocken Books, 1985) in The Abbeville Review, https://www.abbevilleinstitute.org/review/historical-consciousness, accessed February 12, 2019. Dr. Wilson taught in the History Department at the University of South Carolina for over 30 years. He is primary editor of *The Papers of John C. Calhoun* and author or editor of over 30 books and over 600 articles, essays and reviews.

> rectified, their attacks become
> fiercer, their complaints more
> numerous, . . .[45]

Somebody needs to tell race-obsessed academia that this is 2022 and not 1922 or 1822. We have had a Civil Rights Movement in America. There is unlimited opportunity for everybody. If you fail in America, it's your own fault.

There is not a single law in the entire country discriminating against non-whites because of skin color, which is why millions break our laws every month to come here.

In fact, there is often discrimination against whites and Asians in such things as college admissions (of course, where else but academia would you find such obvious discrimination).

We don't want academia's identity politics and racist hate like Critical Race Theory, or the news media's fake history like the *1619 Project*.

The primary theme of the *1619 Project* is that the American Revolutionary War was fought because the British were about to abolish slavery. That is a complete fraud, an invention without a shred of evidence. Not a single letter, speech, document, nothing.

---

[45] James S. Robbins, *Erasing America, Losing Our Future by Destroying Our Past* (Washington, DC: Regnery Publishing, 2018), 3.

Peter W. Wood states in *1620, A Critical Response to the 1619 Project*:

> The *1619 Project* aligns with the views of those on the progressive left who hate America and would like to transform it radically into a different kind of nation. [46]

Wood points out that Nikole Hannah-Jones, creator of the *1619 Project*, has stated many times her goal is reparations. He concludes there is "only bitterness and anger" in the *1619 Project*, that it "is a bucket lowered into the poisoned well of identity politics."[47]

As a matter of record, the British bought and sold black people legally until 1807, and New Englanders and New Yorkers bought and sold black people legally until 1808.

New Englanders and New Yorkers then carried on an illegal slave trade until well after the War Between the States.

Here's how the 2005 book, *Complicity, How the North Promoted, Prolonged and Profited from Slavery*, written by three New England journal-

---

[46] Peter W. Wood, *1620, A Critical Response to the 1619 Project* (New York: Encounter Books, 2020), 3.
[47] Wood, *1620, A Critical Response to the 1619 Project*, 172.

ists then with the *Hartford Courant*, described New York's illegal slave trade:

> New York City's bustling seaport became the hub of an enormously lucrative illegal slave trade. Manhattan shipyards built ships to carry captive Africans, the vessels often outfitted with crates of shackles and with the huge water tanks needed for their human cargo. A conservative estimate is that during the illegal trade's peak years, 1859 and 1860, at least two slave ships—each built to hold between 600 and 1,000 slaves—left lower Manhattan every month.[48]

W. E. B. Du Bois in his famous book, *The Suppression of the African Slave-Trade to the United States of America 1638-1870,* writes that Boston, New York and Portland, Maine were the largest slave trading ports on the planet in 1862, a year into the War Between the States:

> 'The number of persons engaged in the slave-trade, and the amount of capital embarked in it, exceed our powers of calculation. The city of

---

[48] Farrow, Lang, Frank, *Complicity*, xxviii.

New York has been until of late
[1862] the principal port of the world
for this infamous commerce;
although the cities of Portland and
Boston are only second to her in that
distinction. Slave dealers added
largely to the wealth of our
commercial metropolis; they
contributed liberally to the treasuries
of political organizations, and their
bank accounts were largely depleted
to carry elections in New Jersey,
Pennsylvania, and Connecticut.'[49]

The North's addiction to slave trading
should come as no surprise. Much of the infrastructure of New England and New York was
built with the enormous profits from their slave
trading.

Five out of six New England states were
vigorous slave trading states. Little Rhode Island
was a dynamo and America's transatlantic leader
in the eighteenth century

launching nearly 1,000 voyages to

---

[49] W.E.B. Du Bois, *The Suppression of the African
Slave-Trade to the United States of America, 1638-1870*
(New York: Longmans, Green and Co., 1896), 179. Du
Bois is quoting the *Continental Monthly*, January, 1862,
p. 87, the article "The Slave-Trade in New York."

Africa and carrying at least
100,000 captives back across the
Atlantic. The captains and crews of
these ships were often the veteran
seamen of America: New
Englanders.[50]

Rhode Island's Reverend Samuel Hopkins
admits the slave trade was Newport, Rhode
Island's "first wheel of commerce" but it was not
just Newport's first wheel of commerce, it was
all of New England and New York's first wheel
of commerce:

> 'The inhabitants of Rhode Island,
> especially those of Newport, have
> had by far the greater share of this
> traffic, of all these United States.
> This trade in human species has
> been the first wheel of commerce
> in Newport, on which every other
> movement in business has chiefly
> depended.'[51]

Another famous Rhode Island slave trader,
John Brown, whose family founded Brown University, said in a Providence newspaper in 1789:

---

[50] Farrow, Lang, Frank, *Complicity*, xxviii.
[51] Farrow, Lang, Frank, *Complicity*, 99-100.

'there was no more crime in
bringing off a cargo of slaves than
in bringing off a cargo of
jackasses.'[52]

Like the drug trade today, the slave trade
was lucrative. When you can buy a slave in Africa — perhaps a warrior that had himself been
on a mission to capture slaves but instead got
captured — for $50 and sell him for $1,000, that
is a huge profit even today, much less back
then.[53]

Harvard professor, Bernard Bailyn, "dean of
colonial historians," wrote:

[T]he main factor in New
England's phenomenal economic
success, 'the key dynamic force,'
was slavery.[54]

Black tribal chieftains in Africa were the
starting point of global slavery and the African
diaspora. For centuries, slaves were Africa's
chief export. They were the unfortunate captives

---

[52] John Brown, in *United States Chronicle*, March 26,
1789, in Farrow, Lang, Frank, *Complicity*, 110.
[53] Farrow, Lang, Frank, *Complicity*, 126.
[54] Farrow, Lang, Frank, *Complicity*, 48.

of tribal warfare, gathered up and waiting in around 40 slave forts built by the British and other Europeans up and down the African coast because they needed labor in their colonies.

Harvard historian Henry Louis Gates, Jr. in a *New York Times* article, "Ending the Slavery Blame-Game," quotes Boston University historians John Thornton and Linda Heywood who estimated "that 90 percent of those shipped to the New World were enslaved by Africans and then sold to European traders."

Gates gets into specifics:

> [T]he sad truth is that the
> conquest and capture of Africans
> and their sale to Europeans was
> one of the main sources of foreign
> exchange for several African
> kingdoms for a very long time.
> Slaves were the main export of the
> kingdom of Kongo; the Asanta
> Empire in Ghana exported slaves
> and used the profits to import
> gold. Queen Njinga, the brilliant
> 17th-century monarch of the
> Mbundu, waged wars of resistance
> against the Portuguese but also
> conquered polities as far as 500
> miles inland and sold her captives

to the Portuguese. When Njinga
converted to Christianity, she sold
African traditional religious
leaders into slavery, claiming that
they had violated her new
Christian precepts.[55]

Gates writes about the shocking but admirable display by some African leaders today who have begged African Americans to forgive them for selling their ancestors into slavery:

In 1999, for instance, President
Mathieu Kerekou of Benin
astonished an all-black
congregation in Baltimore by
falling to his knees and begging
African-Americas' forgiveness for
the "shameful" and "abominable"
role Africans played in the trade.
Other African leaders, including
Jerry Rawlings of Ghana, followed
Mr. Kerekou's bold example.[56]

---

[55] Henry Louis Gates, Jr., "Ending the Slavery Blame-Game," the *New York Times*, April 22, 2010, https://www.nytimes.com/2010/04/23/opinion/23gates.html, accessed 5-21-22.
[56] Ibid.

Captives in Africa were held sometimes for months, chained and shackled in pens inside slave forts on Africa's coast, waiting for European, New York and New England slave traders.

They would then be placed into the bowels of scorching hot slave ships that were filled to capacity with Africans on their backs, chained side by side to the decks below, where there was no ventilation, no fresh air.

Poor slaves had to endure the stench of vomit, urine, feces and death cooked together in ovenlike heat for months through the Middle Passage. No description of Hell could be worse than a New England or New York slave ship, or a British or Portuguese or Spanish slave ship before them.

The North, especially New England and New York, with Europeans, own the cruelty and brutality of the slave trade, which was more brutal than slavery itself because slave traders did not have to live with their slaves. All they had to do was deliver them and collect their money.

In the American slave trade, New England and New York own the stench and horror of slavery's Middle Passage.

Academia may be shocked to find out but nobody was disappointed that slavery was over, though it was not yet over for three of the six Union slave states that had slavery months after the war, until the Thirteenth Amendment ended it in December, 1865.

As Lincoln himself said, he didn't know how to end slavery and if he had been born into it as Southerners were, he would do no different than they.

Southerners would have unquestionably ended slavery in a better way than what happened with almost a million blacks dying from disease and exposure after the War Between the States[57] followed by a century of second class citizenship. It was in the South's best interest to end slavery with peace, opportunity and good will for all.

Slavery existed in the South but blacks and whites did not hate each other. They got along better than anywhere in America, as Alexis de Tocqueville noted, because the South was a biracial nation. There were more free blacks in the South, around 250,000, out of their population of nine million, than there were black people in the entire North out of their population of twenty-two million.

---

[57] Jim Downs, *Sick from Freedom, African-American Illness and Suffering During the Civil War and Reconstruction* (Oxford, UK: Oxford University Press, 2012).

What did Northerners know about blacks except that they had made huge fortunes selling them, and they hated them and didn't want them in the North as job competition or in the West as neighbors.

Literary colossus Charles Dickens, in addition to his many novels and short stories, published a periodical, *All the Year Round*. He was on top of current events and our American war. Dickens wrote:

> Every reasonable creature may know, if willing, that the North hates the Negro, and that until it was convenient to make a pretence that sympathy with him was the cause of the War, it hated the abolitionists and derided them up hill and down dale.[58]

Jim Crow was born in the North as C. Vann Woodward states in *The Strange Career of Jim Crow,* and he lived in the North a long time before moving South.

All nations ended slavery with gradual,

---

[58] Charles Dickens, letter to W. W. De Cerjat 16 March 1862, in Graham Storey, ed., *The Letters of Charles Dickens* (Oxford: Clarendon Press, 1998), Vol. Ten, 1862-1864, 53-54.

compensated emancipation and we could have too but there was no plan by virtue signaling abolitionists, and, of course, there was no offer from the North to contribute from the treasury to buy the freedom of black slaves in the South who would then come North and be job competition.

Several Northern and Western states had laws forbidding blacks from even visiting, much less living there, including Lincoln's Illinois.

Dr. Michael R. Bradley has given us the words of some of the most important participants in the War Between the States at a critical point in American history, when the republic of the Founding Fathers died and the federal government became supreme over the states.

Lee had surrendered and the war was nearly over but units were still on battlefields and had not yet broken up. Not all commanders addressed their men. Many just broke up and started home as best they could.

The seventeen extant farewell addresses Bradley has dug out are an excellent representative for all the other soldiers in the war. They tell us exactly what men on both sides were feeling after all that death and destruction, and why they had fought.

The addresses also talk about the future in

our reunited country.

As one might imagine there was jubilation on the Northern side at their victory, and deep disappointment on the Southern but not despair. There was a manly, dignified acceptance of the loss, and pride in their victories that were more impressive because Southerners were outnumbered four to one by a well-armed, well-fed, well-clothed invader whose army was 25% foreign born, while they, themselves, were often hungry and ragged.

Southerners were ecstatic to fight for their sacred cause of independence and die for it, and hundreds of thousands had.

Basil Gildersleeve, a Confederate soldier from Charleston, South Carolina, states well the feeling in the hearts of the Southerners. He wrote this in his book, *The Creed of the Old South,* published 27 years after the war:

> All that I vouch for is the feeling; . . .
> there was no lurking suspicion of
> any moral weakness in our cause.
> Nothing could be holier than the
> cause, nothing more imperative
> than the duty of upholding it. There
> were those in the South who, when
> they saw the issue of the war, gave
> up their faith in God, but not their

faith in the cause.[59]

One of the best orations was given by perhaps the greatest soldier of the War Between the States on either side, Confederate Lieutenant General Nathan Bedford Forrest, who is often attacked by academia's jealous, politicized historians, but his address, like his deeds and life, is towering and speaks for itself.

One of the sweetest and saddest was from Confederate Major General Robert F. Hoke who writes that the Southern "star has set in blood, but yet in glory."

The address by the white officer, Lieutenant Colonel Charles Tyler Trowbridge of the United States Colored Troops, from Morris Island in Charleston where they were stationed, is fascinating. Bradley gives us much detail about the USCT. Black units were always commanded by white officers because blacks were not permitted to rise higher than sergeant. Often black troops and officers were looked down on by other Union soldiers. Nathan Bedford Forrest is often accused of atrocities at Fort Pillow but the

---

[59] Basil L. Gildersleeve, *The Creed of the Old South*, Baltimore: The Johns Hopkins Press, 1915; reprint: BiblioLife, Penrose Library, University of Denver (no date given), 26-27. Gildersleeve was known as one of the greatest classical scholars of all time, perhaps the greatest.

USCT has a record of the same type atrocities during the attack on Petersburg, Virginia in 1864. Bradley points out that many of the Union's black troops were not volunteers but were rounded up and coerced, or a "loyal" (Union) slaveholder would enlist his slave and receive the enlistment bonus. Trowbridge, himself, was arrested and court-martialed for murder in Newberry, South Carolina but found "not guilty" by a friendly court, which brought a harsh rebuke from Major General Charles Devens who had brought the charges against him. Despite often poor officers, Bradley writes that the USCT "generally" fought well as noted by a Confederate officer paying his enemy a compliment at the Battle of Nashville.

Michael Bradley is a distinguished historian with an impressive educational background including an M.A. and Ph.D. from Vanderbilt University. See "About the Author" for a complete biography.

He is from the Tennessee-Alabama state line region near Fayetteville, Tennessee and his love of home and its history are obvious and a pleasure to read. One always writes best on what one loves most and is most fascinated by.

Many of his books are about the War Between the States in Tennessee, or Nathan Bedford Forrest and his men, but he has written on topics ranging from the Revolutionary War to death in the Great Smoky Mountains.

He taught United States History at Motlow College near Tullahoma, Tennessee for thirty-six years.

In 1994 he was awarded the Jefferson Davis Medal in Southern History, and in 2006 he was elected commander of the Tennessee Division, SCV. He was also appointed to Tennessee's Civil War Sesquicentennial Commission.

Michael Bradley has given us biographical information on the seventeen commanders giving the farewell addresses, and exciting narrative history researched in minute detail on each unit and their battles. If you love history, it does not get better than this.

You will thoroughly enjoy this book and learn a great deal about why men on both sides fought in the War Between the States and what they planned to do afterward.

I am very proud to be Michael Bradley's publisher and friend.

Gene Kizer, Jr.
May 10, 2022

The Last Words

Introduction

The emphasis on slavery, only, as the cause of the War Between the States, has led to the creation of a fairy tale entitled the "Myth of the Holy Cause." The North is awarded the moral high ground for supposedly fighting to end slavery and the South is condemned. This view is historically incorrect.

Tennessee provides a good illustration of the fatally flawed "single cause" argument. In February, 1861, Governor Isham Harris toured the state of Tennessee urging people to vote to secede in order to protect slavery. The vote was a resounding defeat for Harris and his supporters. By a large margin Tennesseans voted to remain in the Union and did not change their minds until June, 1861, when the war was several weeks into its progress. The issue which changed the minds of Tennessee voters was whether or not to send men to assist the Lincoln administration to put down "a domestic insurrection." Similar conditions caused Arkansas, North Carolina, and Virginia to stand with Tennessee in refusing to secede over the single issue of slavery.

71

Another favorite piece of evidence used by those who advocate for slavery as the single cause of the war is the "Cornerstone Speech" of Alexander Hamilton Stephens, vice president of the Confederacy. There is a problem right off the bat with the Cornerstone Speech because there is no official version approved and signed-off-on by Stephens. It was an extemporaneous speech given in Savannah, Georgia on March 21, 1861, three weeks before the war began. Some people in the audience took notes and that is the basis of our knowledge about the speech.

The speech, as it has come down to us, before even mentioning slavery, goes into great detail on the many economic issues that enriched the North at the expense of the South such as protective tariffs that the South outlawed in its constitution. It is a deeply philosophical speech by one of the greatest thinkers of the time extolling the virtues of the new Southern republic that is now improved by removing the issues of contention that had rankled North and South for a half century.

He does state that slavery is the cornerstone of the new government and that slavery is the African's "natural and normal condition."

That's all single-cause advocates need to hear. Nothing else matters. It does not matter that Stephens also stated that Northerners "are disinclined to give up the benefits they derive from slave labor," especially the "collection of taxes raised by slave labor." That somehow does not raise questions about the North's large part in encouraging slavery, and before that, their near exclusive carrying on of the American slave trade. To single cause advocates, the Confederate vice president has spoken therefore the entire Confederate enterprise is nothing but an attempt to preserve and spread slavery.

When the United States was preparing to go to war in Iraq in 2001, Vice President Richard Cheney said the cause of the war was "weapons of mass destruction" in the hands of the Iraqi government. Did Cheney's statement establish the cause of the war with Iraq as WMDs, even though no such weapons were ever found?

More importantly, did he speak for the United States of America and posterity or did he speak for himself? If Cheney spoke only for himself, then we must accept that Stephens did too, if those in the audience taking notes have passed along to us a true representation of Stephens's talk.

Besides, if we are to accept the word of Alexander Stephens as the truth of history, then we must accept the right of secession and sovereignty of the states - States' Rights - because he makes those arguments too, and brilliantly, in his two-volume, 800 page epic, *A Constitutional View of the Late War Between the States; Its Causes, Character, Conduct and Results.*

There is also the question, did soldiers, North and South, fight over slavery?

James M. McPherson answers that question in two books, *What They Fought For: 1861-1865* and *For Cause & Comrades: Why Men Fought In The Civil War.*[60] He found that the soldiers who fought did not see slavery as their reason for fighting. He points out that only 10% of the Confederate letters he examined mentioned slavery at all, while only 5% of Union letters expressed opposition to slavery. The farewell addresses in this book back that up.

As recently as the 1970's, most historians argued that there were multiple causes for the war. The idea that such a vast conflagration could be caused by a single issue was held to be ridiculous. States' Rights, tariffs and other economic factors were considered, social differences and attitudes toward life were thought significant. In short, many things contributed to the simmering controversy.

Contemporary historians have not disproved

---

[60] James M. McPherson, *What They Fought For: 1861-1865 (*New York: Random House, 1994); *For Cause & Comrades: Why Men Fought In The Civil War (*New York: Oxford University Press, 1997).

the multi-cause argument, they simply refuse to consider it. They argue that their interpretation is right because they say so and nothing else matters. It makes no difference that historians can and do change their minds as new evidence and interpretations come to light.

A century-and-a-half earlier, in the 1870's and '80's, the veterans of the war agreed among themselves that the South had fought for States' Rights and the North for preservation of the Union.

But some historians today assert that the veterans who fought the war did not know what they were talking about, and that they did not choose to give an accurate account of why they fought.

Nevermind that anyone touring a battlefield cannot find a single monument to Union soldiers which boasts that the men fought to end slavery. They all honor the bravery of those who fought and died, and speak of preserving the Union. Perhaps this emphasis on preserving the Union is why historians almost always call the United States forces the "Union Army" despite the fact that this name displaces slavery as the central factor supposedly causing the war.

Those same historians argue that Union veterans agreed to the "States' Rights/Preservation of the Union" narrative during a "period of reconciliation" when there was a desire to reunite the nation. Apparently it is not realized by those presenting this argument that reconciliation shows the Northern motive *was* to preserve the Union. The Union had been saved, now the veterans wanted to restore it by reconciling North and South. Clearly, slavery was not why the vast majority of Union veterans fought.

In 1860, the South did not need to secede in order to be a slaveholding republic. The South was already a member of a slaveholding republic named the United States of America.

Not only was slaveholding a fact of life in the United States, the institution was firmly protected by the Constitution. The Supreme Court had ruled in the *Dred Scott* case that "neither the Congress nor the President can end slavery." Such action could be taken only by a state. With the South in the Union, no constitutional amendment could have received the necessary number of votes to end slavery, and neither would new justices likely have been appointed to the Supreme Court who favored overturning *Scott*.

Remember, the Corwin Amendment passed the United States Congress, was strongly supported by Abraham Lincoln, and was approved by five Union states before the war made it moot. It would have enshrined slavery into the

Constitution forever had Lincoln and the North gotten their way early on.

No one was attempting to end slavery in 1860 except for a small band of abolitionists who were hated in the North. To view secession as a move intended to protect slavery from an imminent threat is to ignore the facts. There was no serious threat to slavery in 1860.

Often cited is the desire of the Republican Party to keep slavery out of the western territories. This stand was not anti-slavery. It was anti-black. The West, Lincoln and others argued, should be open to white men only.

Laws in Ohio, Indiana, Illinois, Iowa and other states including several in the West such as Oregon, denied free people of color the right to live in those states.

The 1863 Homestead Act, passed by Congress and signed by Lincoln the same year the Emancipation Proclamation was issued, opened up the West but limited settlement to citizens. African Americans were not citizens in 1863. Republicans put a "whites only" sign in front of the little house on the prairie. This is what the Republican Party meant by "keeping slavery out of the western territories."

Unknown to most historians is a series of resolutions issued by 10 Northern states in January 1861 as the secession crisis swept the nation. The legislatures of New York, New Jersey, Pennsylvania, Ohio, Minnesota, Wisconsin, Michigan, Massachusetts, Indiana and Maine issued resolutions condemning, not slavery, but secession, and pledging themselves to raise troops to restore the Union.

These resolutions speak of the prosperity brought by the Union, implying an economic reason for their stand, and Minnesota said plainly that Union control of the Mississippi River was necessary for their economy to flourish.

New Jersey and Ohio do mention slavery and both support it. New Jersey called for a constitutional amendment which would perpetuate slavery, and Ohio said the matter should be left up to individual states. There is no suggestion of a "holy war to make men free."

The view of Abraham Lincoln was clear. In his first inaugural address he stated that he had no intention of interfering with slavery where it existed. As stated, Lincoln supported the Corwin Amendment, which would have embodied slavery in the fundamental document of the nation. That was a much stronger protection for slavery than the *Dred Scott* decision.

In his call for troops in 1861, Lincoln said nothing about ending slavery but spoke only of putting down a domestic insurrection.

But, then, of course Lincoln wouldn't say anything about ending slavery because when he called for 75,000 volunteers to invade the South, there were more slave states in the Union than in the Confederacy. There were eight slave states in the Union, soon to be increased by one with the admission of West Virginia as a slave state in 1863, ironically just weeks after the Emancipation Proclamation was issued. There were only seven slave states in the Confederacy.

In the Preliminary Emancipation Proclamation, September, 1862, Lincoln told the South that if they ended the war and returned to the Union within ninety days they could keep their slaves. Slavery would end in Confederate territory only if the South insisted on continuing its fight for independence.

Of course, Southerners *did* continue their fight for independence, which proves they were not fighting for slavery but independence.

The Preliminary Emancipation Proclamation also said the search would continue for a place outside of the United States to send the newly freed blacks to, since they could not live here.

The statement that the war was caused by secession is dismissed by most contemporary historians as part of "the Myth of the Lost Cause." What to current historians is a myth was to Lincoln and his contemporaries, a reality. Had there been no secession there would have been no war. No responsible person in the North was prepared to start a war to end slavery in 1860 with the Northern economy totally dependent on Southern cotton.

Had the Southern states not seceded, slavery would have continued in the United States and likely died a natural death within a generation as technology to pick cotton improved. The only reason for slavery was to get the cotton picked. Southerners would much rather be like Northerners, and hire and fire as business dictated without slavery's birth-to-death commitment.

For most people in 1860, North and South, slavery was not a moral question but a political and economic one.

Secession was not a move to protect slavery nor to perpetuate slavery. Those goals could have been achieved by remaining in the Union.

Secession was the disgust of Southerners with the murderers and terrorists like John Brown that Northerners sent into the South to rape and kill Southerners.

Secession was the disgust of Southerners with the political hatred Northerners had piled on them so Republicans could rally their votes to win the 1860 election and take over the government.

Most of all, secession was the desire of Southerners to be independent and govern themselves. In the South, 1861 was 1776 all over.

Only God knows the exact cause of the war but we can get closer to the truth by reading the words of the men who fought the war.

Right after Lee's surrender, with armies still facing each other in the field, many officers wrote farewell addresses to their men. In those last words, they reviewed the record they and their men had produced and they expressed their ideas as to why the war had been fought. Surprisingly, not all high-ranking officers wrote these addresses. Some just went home.

Among those who did write a farewell address are commanders of armies, brigades, regiments, and companies. They viewed the war from a variety of perspectives and they spoke before later events and the passage of time obscured their minds.

Their emotions are genuine and real. They are not influenced by myths or fairy tales surrounding their actions, or by the political passions of Reconstruction and reunification, or by the politicization of history.

Historians of the past and those who lived through the war reached a far different conclusion than today's Woke historians and news media.

An accurate understanding of the cause of the war is to be found in the minds of those who wrote farewell addresses while still on the field of battle. They knew what they had fought for, and said it clearly.

Why use the title *The Last Words*?

The men who fought the War Between the States formed an unbreakable bond of love and brotherhood which lasted for the rest of their lives. Many had come from the same towns and counties, fought in units made up of neighbors and relatives, and grieved and died as kin.

When the war ended, both victors and vanquished knew an important chapter in American history had closed. They knew most would not meet again in this life.

These are the last words they would speak, soldier to soldier.

Michael R. Bradley
Tullahoma, Tennessee
February, 2021

The Farewell Addresses

Here are seventeen farewell addresses of Union and Confederate commanders to their men while still on the battlefield at the very end of the War Between the States, with biographies of the commanders, and unit histories and battles.

There are eight Confederate and nine Union, starting with Confederate General Robert E. Lee's *General Orders No. 9*.

The addresses mostly alternate between Confederate and Union, though, because of the odd number and desire to pair up some of the addresses, there are two Union addresses in a row in two places.

General Robert E. Lee

General Orders, No. 9
Address to the Army of Northern Virginia, CSA

April 10, 1865

General Robert E. Lee in 1863. Photographer unknown.

Hd. Qrs. Army of N. Va.
General Orders
No. 9

After four years of arduous service
marked by unsurpassed courage and
fortitude, the Army of Northern Virginia
has been compelled to yield to
overwhelming numbers and resources.

I need not tell the brave survivors of
so many hard fought battles, who have
remained steadfast to the last, that I have
consented to this result from no distrust of
them; but feeling that valor and devotion
could accomplish nothing that could
compensate for the loss that must have
attended the continuance of the contest, I
determined to avoid the useless sacrifice of
those whose past services have endeared
them to their countrymen.

By the terms of the agreement,
officers and men can return to their homes
and remain until exchanged. You will take
with you the satisfaction that proceeds
from the consciousness of duty faithfully
performed; and I earnestly pray that a
Merciful God will extend to you His
blessing and protection. With an

unceasing admiration of your constancy and devotion to your Country, and a grateful remembrance of your kind and generous consideration for myself, I bid you all an affectionate farewell.

R.E. Lee, Genl.[61]

Robert Edward Lee took command of the Confederate army defending Richmond in the spring of 1862 following the wounding of Joseph E. Johnston at the Battle of Fair Oaks. Almost immediately, Lee changed the name of his command to the Army of Northern Virginia, and, as such, it would win enduring fame as a staunch military organization. Within a few weeks the men of the ANVa, as it was styled in dispatches, formed a personal bond with their commanding officer, a bond more intense than that shared by the soldiers of any other command with their leader.

The confidence of the soldiers of the Army of Northern Virginia in their general was unbounded. If Lee—"Marse Robert" was their

---

[61] Douglas Southall Freeman, *R. E. Lee: A Biography*, 4 vols. (New York: Charles Scribner's Sons, 1936), Vol. 4, 154-55.

affectionate nickname for him—said "do this," they did it without question, confident that their well-being and the success of their cause required it.

Lee was a realist and had told the Confederate government many months before that if the struggle became a siege of Petersburg and Richmond, the war would be lost. The South simply did not have the resources to win a protracted fight of that nature. Still, Lee and his men endured, looking for any opening to avoid the seemingly inevitable.

On April 9, 1865, the inevitable became reality. Following a brief exchange of notes, Lee met with Ulysses S. Grant, commander of all U.S. forces, at the house of Wilmer McLean at Appomattox Court House and signed the terms of surrender, which ended the existence of the Army of Northern Virginia. That same night Lee instructed his adjutant, Colonel Charles Marshall, to write an order to the army bidding them farewell. The address written by Marshall reflects the grace and style of writing produced by a classical education as well as the directness expected in a military communication.

On the morning of April 10, the weather was rainy and a constant stream of visitors to Lee's headquarters tent prevented Marshall from concentrating on his task. About ten o'clock, Lee ordered Marshall to get into Lee's personal ambulance so he could work without interruption. When the first draft, in pencil, was finished, it was taken to Lee who struck out an entire paragraph, made one or two other minor changes, and then instructed Marshall to have it copied in ink with copies going to all Corps commanders. These were all signed in person by Lee and then issued to the appropriate officers. During the day many people made their own copies and brought them to Lee and he signed many of them.

The "original" of General Orders, No. 9 was the pencil draft which Lee amended and it was most certainly destroyed when the copies in ink were made. There is no record of the contents of the paragraph Lee edited out of Marshall's first draft but one may assume Lee thought it might encourage continued bitter feeling. President John F. Kennedy admired Lee for that sentiment when he wrote:

> [A]s a New Englander, I recognize
> that the South is still the land of
> Washington, who made our
> Nation - of Jefferson, who shaped
> its direction - and of Robert E. Lee
> who, after gallant failure, urged
> those who had followed him in

bravery to reunite America in
purpose and courage.[62]

"General Orders, No. 9" became a regular
part of the meetings of the United Confederate
Veterans, especially those "Bivouacs," as the
local groups were styled, made up of veterans of
the Army of Northern Virginia. A hundred years
later, at the time of the Civil War Centennial, a
direct descendant of Robert E. Lee made a recording of the farewell address. This recording
was released at Appomattox on April 10, 1965.

In the opening decades of the twenty-first
century, the character and reputation of Lee
have come under attack. It has been alleged that
Lee lost the war for the South because he was
too aggressive, losing lives in attacks instead of
husbanding his numbers. Such criticism ignores
the military realities of the situation. It may
sound wise to remain on the defensive until
one's opponent makes a mistake and only then
attack. But, what if one's opponent does not

---

[62] John F. Kennedy, *Speech of Senator John F. Kennedy*, Raleigh, NC, September 17, 1960, Coliseum
Online by Gerhard Peters and John T. Woolley, The
American Presidency Project,
https://www.presidency.ucsb.edu/documents/speech-
senator-john-f-kennedy-raleigh-nc-coliseum, accessed
5/3/2020.

make a major mistake that would allow for a successful attack? The point to be defended will be lost. Joseph Johnston used the "passive-aggressive" model in the Atlanta Campaign and every reader of the history of the war knows how that ended. Lee had little choice but to aggressively make his openings.

Much has been made of late that Lee owned slaves. That is not true. Lee was made the executor of the will of his father-in-law, George Washington Parke Custis, grandson of Martha Washington and step-grandson and adopted son of George Washington. Custis was the owner of the Arlington Estate, which he passed to his daughter, Mary Anna, wife of Robert E. Lee. Today, that estate is our nation's most sacred burial ground: Arlington National Cemetery.

As executor,[63] Lee was responsible for the

---

[63] According to FindLaw, the world's leader in online legal information for consumers and small businesses, here's what the executor of a will does: "By definition, an executor is entrusted with the large responsibility of making sure a person's last wishes are granted with regard to the disposition of their property and possessions. / When it boils down to essentials, an executor of a will is responsible for making sure that any debts and creditors that the deceased had are paid off, and that any remaining money or property is distributed according to their wishes." See https://estate.findlaw.com/estate-administration/what-does-an-executor-do.html, accessed May 10, 2020.

settlement of Custis's will, and among Custis's possessions were slaves. The executor is not the owner of Custis's property. Lee, like all responsible executors, carried out the stipulations of the will he was executing. These stipulations included the provision that all the Arlington slaves be set free within five years. Lee did this, completing the process in 1862. Lee had labeled slavery a moral problem in 1856 but he saw no ready solution to the matter. At any rate, being administrator of the will of his father-in-law does not make Lee the "owner" of his father-in-law's slaves.

Lee has also been accused of fostering the rise of the "Myth of the Lost Cause" and is claimed to have begun this process in his farewell address. Although called a myth, there is a great deal of truth in the arguments presented under the name "Lost Cause."

The "Lost Cause" argues that secession, not slavery, caused the war. This is true. If no Southern state had left the Union, who, in the North, would have called for a war to end slavery? The answer is obvious.

This so-called myth argues that the war was fought over States' Rights, i.e., state sovereignty and supremacy over the Federal Government, which had been created as the agent of the states for certain highly limited purposes of government. This was the belief of the Founding Fathers and it is clearly proclaimed in the secession documents of the Southern States. Most foreigners such as Alexis de Tocqueville, Charles Dickens, and the British historian, Sir John Dalberg Acton,[64] later Lord Acton, agreed. Acton wrote this to Lee a year-and-a-half after Appomattox:

> Without presuming to decide the
> purely legal question, on which it
> seems evident to me from
> Madison's and Hamilton's papers
> that the Fathers of the
> Constitution were not agreed, I
> saw in State Rights the only
> availing check upon the
> absolutism of the sovereign will,
> and secession filled me with hope,
> not as the destruction but as the
> redemption of Democracy. . . .
> Therefore I deemed that you were

---

[64] John Emerich Edward Dalberg Acton, 1st Baron Acton (born 1834, died 1902), is perhaps best known for the aphorism "Power tends to corrupt, and absolute power corrupts absolutely." See his biography at https://www.britannica.com/biography/John-Emerich-Edward-Dalberg-Acton-1st-Baron-Acton, accessed May 3, 2020.

> fighting the battles of our liberty,
> our progress, and our civilization;
> and I mourn for the stake which
> was lost at Richmond more deeply
> than I rejoice over that which was
> saved at Waterloo.[65]

Not surprisingly, States' Rights had recently been upheld by the Supreme Court in the *Dred Scott Case* (1857) with respect to slavery.

The point at which Lee is accused specifically of fostering the Lost Cause position is "compelled to yield to overwhelming numbers and resources." A look at the 1860 census of the United States shows that Lee was right. The population of the nation in that year was 31,443,321. Of this number 22,000,000 (round figures) lived in the states which remained in the Union, 9,000,000 in the states which seceded. Of the 9,000,000 people in the South almost 4,000,000 were slaves. While the African American population gave strength to the Southern economy and war effort through its labor, it was not a major source of manpower for the armies although some free people of color be-

---

[65] John Dalberg Acton to Gen. Robert E. Lee, November 4, 1866, The Acton-Lee Correspondence, https://www.lewrockwell.com/2017/09/no_author/famed-libertarian-writes-robert-e-lee, accessed May 3, 2020.

came Confederate soldiers. The 5,000,000 white population was divided in its loyalties and a significant number of white Southerners joined the U.S. forces.

So, in critical manpower, it was over 22,000,000 white Northerners versus less than 5,000,000 white Southerners. Obviously, the South did face overwhelming numbers. This does not detract from the military accomplishments of the U.S. Army but it does show the "Lost Cause Myth" is no myth.

Lee also had a very clear grasp of the infrastructure which supported both armies. The 1860 census shows that 80% of the country's manufacturing and most of the existing railroad mileage were in states that remained in the Union. The United States also had a stable monetary system based on bullion and a well-functioning government that had been in place for over 60 years. It had an army, navy, merchant marine fleet and relationships with most of the governments of the world.

The South had none of that. The South did not expect war when they seceded. They expected to go on peacefully in their new republic that derived its "just powers from the consent of the governed" as the Declaration of Independence established in 1776. When it became obvious that they were not going to be able to leave in peace, they had to start everything from scratch.

In addition to the North's greater than four-to-one advantage in white population, it also had a pipeline to the wretched refuse of the world with which to feed Union armies continually. While 25% of the Union army were foreign-born immigrants, James McPherson points out that 30% of military age men in the Union states were foreign-born, thus the 25% in the Union army underrepresented the general foreign-born population in the North.[66]

This may be true but later in the war, when enlistments were low and a real problem for both sides, lavish financial inducements and bounties brought tens of thousands of foreigners into the Union army. All total, "a half-billion dollars" was spent by the North on bounties, and "the conscription-substitute-bounty system produced three-quarters of a million new men." Many foreigners had come for the express purpose of "joining the army to cash in on bounties or substitute fees."[67]

The South had no such pipeline of manpower at this critical hour with its money vir-

---

[66] James M. McPherson, *Battle Cry of Freedom: The Civil War Era* (New York: Oxford University Press, 1988), 606.

[67] McPherson, *Battle Cry of Freedom*, 600-606.

tually worthless and its harbors bottled up by the Union blockade.

The ability to sustain an extended military effort as well as the population to do so, was heavily weighted toward the North. "Overwhelming numbers and resources" is a solid fact, not a myth.

Lee does not deal with the causes of the conflict directly in his farewell address, but, for him, the overriding issue was that of serving his home, his state. That was made clear in 1861 when, after being offered command of the U.S. Army by President Lincoln, he instead resigned and offered his services to Virginia.

The idea that soldiers on both sides saw themselves fighting to defend their homes is born out by James M. McPherson in *For Cause & Comrades: Why Men Fought In The Civil War.* McPherson concludes that slavery was not the issue that caused most men to fight. Protection of home was.[68]

Lee's farewell address acknowledges the great love Lee's men had for their leader, and it shows the love and respect Lee had for his men. They were ready to continue the war despite the odds.

The address is poignant. It reflects the char-

---

[68] McPherson, *For Cause & Comrades*, 6.

acter of the man who issued it, a man who was strong but humble and who thought "duty" the most sublime word in the English language.

Like President Kennedy, President Dwight D. Eisenhower had great respect for Gen. Lee and appreciated his efforts to bind up the nation's wounds after its bloodiest war. On August 9, 1960, Eisenhower answered an angry letter from a New York dentist, Dr. Leon W. Scott, who had written eight days earlier and questioned why he kept a picture of Gen. Lee in his White House office.

Dr. Scott wrote:

> I do not understand how any
> American can include Robert E.
> Lee as a person to be emulated,
> and why the President of the
> United States of America should
> do so is certainly beyond me.
>
> The most outstanding thing that
> Robert E. Lee did, was to devote
> his best efforts to the destruction
> of the United States Government,
> and I am sure that you do not say
> that a person who tries to destroy
> our Government is worthy of

being held as one of our heroes.[69]

President Eisenhower wrote:

Dear Dr. Scott:

Respecting your August 1 inquiry calling attention to my often expressed admiration for General Robert E. Lee, I would say, first, that we need to understand that at the time of the War between the States the issue of secession had remained unresolved for more than 70 years. Men of probity, character, public standing and unquestioned loyalty, both North and South, had disagreed over this issue as a matter of principle from the day our Constitution was adopted.

General Robert E. Lee was, in my estimation, one of the supremely gifted men produced by our

---

[69] Dwight D. Eisenhower in Defense of Robert E. Lee, August 10, 2014, Mathew W. Lively, https://www.civilwarprofiles.com/dwight-d-eisenhower-in-defense-of-robert-e-lee/, accessed 5-3-20.

Nation. He believed unswervingly
in the Constitutional validity of his
cause which until 1865 was still an
arguable question in America; he
was a poised and inspiring leader,
true to the high trust reposed in
him by millions of his fellow
citizens; he was thoughtful yet
demanding of his officers and
men, forbearing with captured
enemies but ingenious,
unrelenting and personally
courageous in battle, and never
disheartened by a reverse or
obstacle. Through all his many
trials, he remained selfless almost
to a fault and unfailing in his faith
in God. Taken altogether, he was
noble as a leader and as a man,
and unsullied as I read the pages
of our history.

From deep conviction, I simply say
this: a nation of men of Lee's
caliber would be unconquerable in
spirit and soul. Indeed, to the
degree that present-day American
youth will strive to emulate his
rare qualities, including his

devotion to this land as revealed in
his painstaking efforts to help heal
the Nation's wounds once the
bitter struggle was over, will be
strengthened and our love of
freedom sustained.

Such are the reasons that I
proudly display the picture of this
great American on my office wall.

Sincerely,
Dwight D. Eisenhower[70]

---

[70] Dwight D. Eisenhower letter, August 9, 1960, to Leon
W. Scott, in "Dwight D. Eisenhower in Defense of Robert
E. Lee," August 10, 2014, Mathew W. Lively,
https://www.civilwarprofiles.com/dwight-d-eisenhower-in-
defense-of-robert-e-lee/, accessed 5-3-20.

General Ulysses S. Grant

*Address to the Soldiers of the Armies of the
United States, USA*

June 2, 1865

**General Ulysses S. Grant, Cold Harbor, 1864, from the
Brady-Handy Collection, Library of Congress (LOC).**

June 2, 1865
By order of General Ulysses S. Grant
Adj. Gen. Office No. 108

Soldiers of the Armies of the United States
by your patriotic devotion to your country
in the hour of danger and alarm, your
magnificent fighting bravery, and
endurance, you have maintained the
supremacy of the Union and the
Constitution, overthrown all armed
opposition to the enforcement of the laws
and of the proclamations forever
abolishing slavery, the cause and pretext
of the Rebellion, and opened the way to the
rightful authorities to restore order and
inaugurate peace on a permanent and
enduring basis on every foot of American
soil. Your marches, sieges, and battles in
distance, duration, resolution, and
brilliancy of results dim the luster of the
world's past military achievements and will
be the patriot's precedent in defense of
liberty and right in all time to come. In
obedience to your country's call you left
your homes and families and volunteered
in its defense. Victory has crowned your
valor and secured the purpose of your

*Address to the Soldiers of the Armies of the
United States, USA*

patriotic hearts. And with the gratitude of
your countrymen and the highest honors a
great and free nation can accord you will
soon be permitted to return to your homes
and your families conscious of having
discharged the highest duty of American
citizens. To achieve these glorious
triumphs and secure to yourselves, your
fellow countrymen, and posterity the
blessings of free institutions, tens of
thousands of your gallant comrades have
fallen and sealed the priceless legacy with
their lives. The graves of these a grateful
nation bedews with tears, honors their
memories, and will ever cherish and
support their stricken families.[71]

Ulysses S. Grant was in New York at the
time the farewell address to the armies
was issued. The author of the address is unknown as is the date of its composition. One
wonders if Grant himself read or edited the text
since it does not bear his signature.

---

[71] John Y. Simon, ed. *Papers of Ulysses Grant,* 31 vols.
(Carbondale: Southern Illinois University Press, 1967),
Vol. 9, 217-18.

Address to the Soldiers of the Armies of the
United States, USA

The War Between the States made Ulysses S. Grant, who was born Hiram Ulysses Grant (and lore has it he was not happy with the initials H.U.G.). He changed his name to Ulysses S. Grant when that name was erroneously put on his West Point application by Ohio Congressman Thomas Hamer who nominated him. The "S" is a lone initial and does not stand for a middle name.[72]

In 1861, Grant was a social and economic failure who held a low-paying job, and that, only thanks to the generosity of his relatives. By 1865, he was a national hero who knew the presidency was his for the asking.

Previously, Grant had an undistinguished career in the U.S. Army, then he tried his hand

---

[72] Hamer thought Grant's middle name was Simpson since that was Grant's mother's maiden name, thus the "S". Some today and in the past have listed Simpson as Grant's middle name but he himself joked with his future wife, Julia Dent, and said in an 1844 letter to her, "Find some name beginning with an "S" for me" because "You know I have an "S" in my name and don't know what it stands for." See "10 Things You May Not Know About Ulysses S. Grant," updated April 7, 2020, at https://www.history.com/news/10-things-you-may-not-know-about-ulysses-s-grant, accessed April 21, 2020; and "Ulysses S. Grant," updated March 30, 2020, at https://www.history.com/topics/us-presidents/ulysses-s-grant-1, accessed April 21, 2020.

as a farmer during which time he owned and rented slaves. He had also been involved in the retail trade. The coming of the war and the demand for men with military experience to command troops gave him the chance for his stubborn persistence to make its mark on history.

Grant made his reputation as commander of U.S. forces in Tennessee and Mississippi during the first three years of the war. His capture of Forts Henry and Donelson in February 1862 made him the first Union hero of the war. This reputation was somewhat tarnished by the Confederate attack on Grant's army at Shiloh, but he managed to repulse the assault with the help of reinforcements from the army led by Don Carlos Buell.

December 1862 saw Grant advancing on Vicksburg only to be forced to retreat when a force of 2,500 Confederate cavalry led by Earl Van Dorn captured and burned his base of supplies at Holly Springs, Mississippi.

Ironically, on the eve of the Emancipation Proclamation, Mrs. Grant, who was present with her husband's army at Holly Springs, was accompanied by one of her four slaves, a woman

named Julia, also called Jule or Black Julia.[73] In
early 1860, just before the Grants were to move
to Galena, Illinois from St. Louis so Ulysses
could work in his father's business, Mrs. Grant
wrote:

---

[73] Mrs. Grant adamantly claimed her whole life that those
four slaves were hers. Supposedly, Black Julia was
given to Mrs. Grant by her father, Frederick Dent, at their
home place White Haven near St. Louis, Missouri the
day she (Mrs. Grant) was born. However, there are no
records of this, just Mrs. Grant's many statements in her
memoirs such as this, in 1858, when the Grants were
planning a move to Kentucky: "In anticipation of this
move, we had sold our farm, horses, farming imple-
ments, and crops. The four slaves we kept."

The Kentucky move never took place but shortly
thereafter they moved into St. Louis and Mrs. Grant
wrote: "We had brought into the city with us the four
servants my father had given me, but these were young,
ranging from eighteen to twelve years of age. They were
born at the old farm and were excellent, though so
young." See Julia Dent Grant, *The Personal Memoirs of
Julia Dent Grant (Mrs. Ulysses S. Grant)*, John Y. Simon,
ed. (Carbondale, Illinois: Southern Illinois University
Press, copyright 1975 by the Ulysses S. Grant Association), 80-81. See also Candice Shy Hooper, "The Two
Julias," February 14, 2013,
https://opinionator.blogs.nytimes.com/2013/02/14/the-
two-julias, accessed April 10, 2020; and Philip Leigh,
February 8, 2019, "Did Ulysses Grant Own and Rent
Slaves?", https://www.abbevilleinstitute.org/blog/did-
ulysses-grant-own-and-rent-slaves, accessed April 9,
2020.

We rented our pretty little home
and hired out our four servants to
persons whom we knew and who
promised to be kind to them. Papa
was not willing they should go
with me to Galena, saying the
place might not suit us after all,
and if I took them they would, of
course, be free, 'and you know,
sister, you cannot do without
servants.' There is not one word of
truth in the statement made by a
late chronicler of General Grant
that he ever offered to sell one of
these dear family servants of mine,
nor in the statement that one of
these girls was left with, or given
to, Mr. Long for debt. Captain
Grant did not owe Mr. Long or
anyone else in Missouri anything
when we left there or at any other
time. Eliza, Dan, Julia, and John
belonged to me up to the time of
President Lincoln's Emancipation
Proclamation. When I visited the
General during the war, I nearly
always had Julia with me as nurse.
She came near being captured at

General Ulysses S. Grant   111
*Address to the Soldiers of the Armies of the
United States, USA*

Holly Springs.[74]

Mrs. Grant is not correct when she stated
"Eliza, Dan, Julia, and John belonged to me up
to the time of President Lincoln's Emancipation
Proclamation." They belonged to her well after
the Emancipation Proclamation because Missouri was a Union slave state, one of six Union
slave states, and the Emancipation Proclamation
did not free any of the slaves in the Union slave
states or already-captured Confederate
territory.[75]

---

[74] Julia Dent Grant, *The Personal Memoirs of Julia Dent
Grant (Mrs. Ulysses S. Grant)*, 82-83.

[75] The six Union slave states, whose slaves were not
freed by the Emancipation Proclamation, are: Maryland,
Missouri, West Virginia, New Jersey, Kentucky and
Delaware.

West Virginia had come into the Union as a slave
state a few months *after* the Emancipation Proclamation
became effective, albeit with a weak plan for gradual
emancipation called the Willey Amendment that freed no
slaves initially, and would have left thousands of slaves
in slavery their entire lives. It would also have left many
others as slaves for 20 years before being freed.

Of the six Union slave states, Maryland, Missouri and
West Virginia ended slavery close to the end of the war.

The other three states kept their slaves eight-and-a-
half months *beyond* the war. The slaves in New Jersey,
Kentucky and Delaware were not freed until the 13th
Amendment took effect in December, 1865. New Jersey

*Address to the Soldiers of the Armies of the
United States, USA*

Grant, himself, only owned one slave, William Jones, and that was when he was farming near St. Louis. Jones gained his freedom in 1859 "for divers[e] good and valuable considerations" before Grant left Missouri to work for his father in Illinois.[76]

Regardless, Ulysses S. Grant's household was slaveholding even as he led United States troops in battle during the War Between the States. Mrs. Grant often traveled with her husband and she was rarely without the slave, Black Julia. That must always have been an interesting scene, the Union general with his wife and her slave. It is a common practice of historians, in evaluating the extent of slaveholding in the antebellum South, to include all members of a family as "slaveholders" no matter who actually owned the slave property, and by that standard,

---

did have a gradual emancipation program in place but there were still a handful of slaves in New Jersey until the 13th Amendment finally freed them.

The 1860 census showed 225,483 slaves in Kentucky, and 1,798 in Delaware, which is a total of 227,281. Some number of slaves close to that 227,281 remained in bondage eight months beyond the end of the War Between the States in those two Union slave states.

[76] Philip Leigh, February 8, 2019, "Did Ulysses Grant Own and Rent Slaves?", previously cited, accessed April 9, 2020.

*Address to the Soldiers of the Armies of the
United States, USA*

Grant was a slaveholder just about the entire
War Between the States. Grant would have been
a slaveholder from August 22, 1848, when he
married Julia Dent, until Missouri abolished
slavery in early 1865.[77]

Grant was successful in besieging and cap-
turing Vicksburg in July 1863. A period of in-
action followed but in November Grant led por-

---

[77] Missouri held a constitutional convention from January
6 to April 8, 1865. An ordinance abolishing slavery was
passed on January 11, 1865. The Missouri Constitution
of 1865 that came out of that convention, later known as
the Drake Constitution because of the influence of Radical Republican Charles D. Drake, abolished slavery,
disenfranchised most non-Unionists and kicked them out
of office, and required an oppressive loyalty oath. It was
also known as the "Draconian Constitution." It was
adopted by the legislature on April 8, 1865, then barely
ratified by the voters on June 6, 1865. Please see Missouri State Archives, Missouri Constitutions, 1820-1945
at http://mdh.contentdm.oclc.org/cdm/landingpage/
collection/p16795coll1, accessed May 5, 2020; An
Ordinance Abolishing Slavery in Missouri,
https://www.sos.mo.gov/CMSImages/MDH/1865Constitu
tionOrdinanceabolishingslaveryinMissouri.pdf, accessed
May 4, 2020; Constitution of 1865 - Drake Constitution,
http://www.civilwarmo.org/educators/resources/info-
sheets/constitution-1865-drake-constitution, accessed
May 5, 2020; Missouri State Archives, Guide to African
American History, https://www.sos.mo.gov/archives/
resources/africanamerican/guide/image005c, accessed
May 4, 2020.

114   General Ulysses S. Grant
*Address to the Soldiers of the Armies of the
United States, USA*

tions of his army to the relief of Union troops trapped in Chattanooga following the Battle of Chickamauga. The Confederate forces were routed at the Battle of Missionary Ridge and Grant was once again the hero of the hour even though the capture of Missionary Ridge had been accomplished by soldiers of the Army of the Cumberland commanded by George Thomas.

In 1864, Grant was transferred to the east and was made commander of all U.S. armies. Instead of occupying an office in Washington, Grant chose to make his headquarters with the Army of the Potomac and act as virtual commander of that army, largely ignoring George G. Meade who was the official commander. As *de facto* commander of the Army of the Potomac, Grant engaged in the Overland Campaign, which consisted of a series of attempts to break through the line held by the Army of Northern Virginia, all of which failed, and the campaign ended with Union troops besieging Petersburg, Virginia.

By April 1865, attrition in Confederate ranks and the growing strength on the Union side broke the Confederate lines and the attempt of the Army of Northern Virginia to unite with the Army of Tennessee was thwarted at Appomattox

Court House. With all roads blocked, Robert E. Lee surrendered to Ulysses S. Grant.

When the surrender of the Confederates was announced the soldiers celebrated the end of the fighting but there is no record of displays of affection offered to Grant. The men under his command had often condemned him as a "butcher" since his strategy of attrition produced a large number of casualties. Grant had the respect of Union soldiers as a man who won victories but he did not have their love. On arrival in the East in 1864, many officers of the Army of the Potomac wondered how Grant would have fared facing the best the Confederacy had to offer. They noted, correctly, that Grant had made his reputation against weak opponents.

Grant's reputation as a man often in trouble had also preceded him. Following the capture of Forts Henry and Donelson, Grant had been removed from active command because of an unauthorized trip outside of his area of command. After Shiloh, he had again been removed from command while being investigated for allowing his army to be surprised by the Confederate attack. Grant's supply base at Holly Springs, Mississippi had been destroyed in December 1862 by Confederate cavalry and he had had to withdraw to Memphis.

This carelessness in protecting his logistics network put the Lincoln administration in peril. Burnside was defeated at Fredericksburg, Grant retreated from Mississippi, and Lincoln issued the Emancipation Proclamation. Had William S. Rosecrans not won a tactical victory at Stones River the string of military defeats would have made the Proclamation look like a desperate measure by a failing president.

Of course, the talk of Grant's binge drinking was well known and stayed with him. The drinking problem was not so great as Grant's critics asserted nor was it absent, as his defenders said, and some still say.

As the Overland Campaign began in the spring of 1864, there was considerable tension between Grant and George G. Meade. Meade, as mentioned earlier, was officially commander of the Army of the Potomac, but Grant, having his headquarters in the field with that force, turned Meade into little more than a conduit through which orders were issued. At the meeting on April 9, 1865 in the McLean house, Meade was conspicuous by his absence. He was neither informed of, nor invited to, the meeting.

On the night of April 9, Grant ordered all bands near his camp to cease playing and all

Address to the Soldiers of the Armies of the
United States, USA

celebrations to stop. Grant had a migraine head-
ache and wanted quiet.

Grant left Appomattox on April 12, not waiting for the ceremonies marking the formal surrender of the Army of Northern Virginia. For the
rest of the month he was busy with wrapping up
the fighting in other areas of the war and cor-
responding with his subordinate generals. Also,
the assassination of Abraham Lincoln on April
14, cast a pall of gloom over the United States.
Dying at the hands of an assassin caused even
the many people who disliked Lincoln to sud-
denly revere him as a hero.

May 23–24 was set as a time of celebration
to mark the end of the war. A grand review of
the armies of the United States was held in
Washington, following which the men rapidly
began to disperse to their homes.

On June 2, Grant's address, titled Order No.
108, was issued by the Office of the Adjutant
General and not signed by Grant. It is interesting that none of the major biographies of Grant
quote his farewell address.

The content of the address reflects the
views of Secretary of War Edwin Stanton and is
celebratory in nature rather than offering any
attempts at reconciliation. For example, the
phrase saying slavery was "the cause and pre-

Address to the Soldiers of the Armies of the
United States, USA

text of the Rebellion" is not consistent for a man whose household was slaveholding throughout the war and who had, a few years earlier, rented slaves, owned a slave, and whose wife often accompanied him to battlefields along with her slave, Black Julia, who was one of the four she owned. Grant had written to Elihu Washburne, August 30, 1863, and opened the letter with "I never was an abolitionist, not even what could be called anti-slavery . . . ".

Today, many historians present Grant as a champion of civil rights because of his work to suppress the Ku Klux Klan. These same historians fail to point out that Grant did nothing to protect the civil rights of Chinese Americans, Hispanic Americans, Native Americans, or his unfortunate problem with the Jews. On December 17, 1862, Grant issued Order No. 11 which stated: "Jews, as a class violating every regulation of trade established by the Treasury Department and also department orders, are hereby expelled from the department within twenty-four hours from the receipt of this order."[78] He was upset about some Northerners

---

[78] United States. 1880. *The War of the Rebellion: a compilation of the official records of the Union and Confederate armies.* Washington: G.P.O. Ser. 1, Vol. 17, Part 2, 425; McPherson, *Battle Cry of Freedom,* 622-23.

and Southerners trading with each other across their respective lines, and he blamed Jews. Lincoln later rescinded the order.

Historian Phil Leigh, author of *U.S. Grant's Failed Presidency*,[79] says that Grant was not concerned about racial equality but wanted

> to gain the political power that a routinely obedient voting bloc could provide to Republican candidates. For example, only a minority of America's whites voted for Grant when he was first elected President in 1868. His 300,000 popular vote majority resulted from winning about 90% of the votes of mostly illiterate ex-slaves.[80]

Grant's concern for civil rights was limited to the one minority group that could be depended upon to deliver the South's electoral

---

[79] Philip Leigh, *U.S. Grant's Failed Presidency* (Columbia, SC: Shotwell Publishing, 2019).

[80] Philip Leigh, February 3, 2018, "President Grant's Doubtful Civil Rights Motives", https://civilwarchat.wordpress.com/2018/02/03/president-grants-doubtful-civil-rights-motives/, accessed April 10, 2020.

votes to the Republican Party.[81]

Order No. 108 makes slavery the cause of the war but Grant's actions in allowing his wife with her slave, Black Julia, to travel, quite often, with the Union army during the war, are contradictory. Grant was comfortable with slavery. He voted Democrat in 1856. The majority of his public statements, before he rejoined the army, focus on preservation of the Union, the exact same position as Abraham Lincoln during the first twenty months of the war.

---

[81] Ibid.

Lt.-Gen. Nathan Bedford Forrest

Address to Forrest's Cavalry Corps, CSA

May 9, 1865

Lt. Gen. Nathan Bedford Forrest of Tennessee, unknown date and author, part of Brady-Handy Collection, LOC.

Soldiers:

By an agreement made between Liet.-Gen. Taylor, commanding the Department of Alabama. Mississippi, and East Louisiana, and Major-Gen. Canby, commanding United States forces, the troops of this department have been surrendered.

I do not think it proper or necessary at this time to refer to causes which have reduced us to this extremity; nor is it now a matter of material consequence to us how such results were brought about. That we are BEATEN is a self-evident fact, and any further resistance on our part would justly be regarded as the very height of folly and rashness.

The armies of Generals LEE and JOHNSTON having surrendered. You are the last of all the troops of the Confederate States Army east of the Mississippi River to lay down your arms.

The Cause for which you have so long and so manfully struggled, and for which you have braved dangers, endured privations, and sufferings, and made so many sacrifices, is today hopeless. The government which we sought to establish and perpetuate, is at an end. Reason dictates and humanity demands that no more blood be shed. Fully realizing and feeling that such is the case, it is your duty and mine to lay down our arms – submit to the "powers that be" – and to aid in restoring peace and establishing law and order throughout the land.

The terms upon which you were surrendered are favorable, and should be satisfactory and acceptable to all. They manifest a spirit of magnanimity and liberality, on the part of the Federal authorities, which should be met, on our part, by a faithful compliance with all the stipulations and conditions therein expressed. As your Commander, I sincerely hope that every officer and soldier of my command will cheerfully obey the orders given, and carry out in good faith all the terms of the cartel.

Those who neglect the terms and refuse to be paroled, may assuredly expect, when arrested, to be sent North and imprisoned. Let those who are absent from their commands, from whatever cause, report at once to this place, or to Jackson, Miss.; or, if too remote from either, to the nearest United States post or garrison, for parole.

Civil war, such as you have just passed through naturally engenders feelings of animosity, hatred, and revenge. It is our duty to divest ourselves of all such feelings; and as far as it is in our power to do so, to cultivate friendly feelings towards those with whom we have so long contended, and heretofore so widely, but honestly, differed. Neighborhood feuds, personal animosities, and private differences should be blotted out; and, when you return home, a manly, straightforward course of conduct will secure the respect of your enemies. Whatever your responsibilities may be to Government, to society, or to individuals meet them like men.

The attempt made to establish a separate and independent Confederation has failed; but the consciousness of having done your duty faithfully, and to the end, will, in some measure, repay for the hardships you have undergone.

In bidding you farewell, rest assured that you carry with you my best wishes for your future welfare and happiness. Without, in any way, referring to the merits of the Cause in which we have been engaged, your courage and determination, as exhibited on many hard-fought fields, has elicited the respect and admiration of friend and foe. And I now cheerfully and gratefully acknowledge my indebtedness to the officers and men of my command whose zeal, fidelity and unflinching bravery have been the great source of my past success in arms.

I have never, on the field of battle, sent you where I was unwilling to go myself; nor would I now advise you to a course which I felt myself unwilling to pursue. You have been good soldiers, you can be good citizens. Obey the laws, preserve your honor, and the Government to which you have surrendered can afford to be, and will be, magnanimous.

N.B. Forrest, Lieut.-General
Headquarters, Forrest's Cavalry Corps
Gainesville, Alabama
May 9, 1865
General Orders No. 22[82]

---

[82] Thomas Jordan and J.P. Pryor, *The Campaigns of General Nathan Bedford Forrest and of Forrest's Cavalry* (New York: Da Capo Press, 1996), 680-82. Originally published 1886.

Nathan Bedford Forrest is the most controversial, and the most misrepresented, general officer of the entire war. He is the man liberal historians love to hate and the man Civil War buffs adore. Forrest is celebrated for his military genius and his intuitive grasp of psychological warfare (keep the scare on 'em) and dammed for his supposed approval of a massacre of African American and white Tennessee Unionists at Fort Pillow and for his presumptive post-war leadership of the Ku Klux Klan. William T. Sherman said, in 1864, "there will never be peace in Tennessee until Forrest is dead." Since controversy and argument still swirl around Forrest it appears he is not deceased!

Forrest grew up on a small farm in Bedford County, Tennessee (his birthplace is now in Marshal County thanks to a redrawing of boundaries) and became "the man of the family" in his early teens when his father died. Later he took the family to Mississippi where he became a successful farmer, businessman, and political leader. He moved to Memphis, engaged in the slave trade, and was elected alderman. By 1860, still in his thirties, he was worth over a million dollars.

Forrest enlisted as a private, was made a lieutenant colonel almost immediately and was instructed to raise a regiment of cavalry. As head of a cavalry force he rose quickly through the ranks to become a lieutenant general before the end of the war. Forrest also established a reputation for hard fighting, beginning with his first encounter of any importance at Sacramento, Kentucky and continuing to his last battle at Selma, Alabama. He also perfected the technique of striking deep behind the Union front line to disrupt lines of supply. The first attempt by Forrest at such raiding came in July 1862 at Murfreesboro, Tennessee on his forty-first birthday. He repeated the tactic in December 1862 by raiding for two weeks into West Tennessee, thoroughly destroying the Mobile & Ohio Railroad which brought supplies to the army of Ulysses S. Grant. By 1864 Forrest had been given an independent command in Mississippi and West Tennessee and there he won some of his most brilliant victories such as Brice's Cross Roads. Two other raids into Middle Tennessee and West Tennessee in 1864 cemented his grasp of raiding.

Forrest spent most of his military career doing traditional cavalry service, scouting and screening the infantry force of the Army of Tennessee. It was in this traditional capacity that he served at Fort Donelson, at Shiloh, and throughout 1863 during the Tullahoma and Chickamauga campaigns.

By the end of the war Forrest was the most feared opponent the Union had in the west and the most celebrated leader in the Confederate ranks. His campaigns are still studied today as early examples of mobile warfare.

Fort Pillow, April 9, 1864, casts a dark shadow over the memory of Forrest. Something happened there which has been exploited but never explained. After an all-day engagement Confederate forces got close enough to the fortifications at Fort Pillow to capture them by storm, doing so only after the Union commander had refused to surrender. In the ensuing chaos of a position captured by direct assault some Union soldiers were killed in a manner which violated the rules of war. The crucial questions of how many such deaths occurred and who is responsible have never been answered, though Forrest, as commanding officer, bears responsibility for the conduct of his troops.

The Fort Pillow affair was immediately exploited by the North. A congressional committee investigated the matter and published a report, of which 40,000 copies were distributed, in which survivors gave graphic reports of men being shot after surrendering. One very obvious problem is that none of these witnesses gave the name of a single person who they saw killed. The men of these units had served together for more than a year, yet no-one recognized a friend, mess mate, or non-commissioned officer who was killed unlawfully. The more serious problem is that the Congressional Report has all the markings of a propaganda piece. The Union cause, militarily and politically, was at a low ebb. The Confederates had taken serious blows in 1863 but they still appeared full of fight. Recruitment in the North was difficult and very large bounties were being offered to lure recruits. The Democratic Party, with its call for peace, appeared to be in good position for the 1864 elections at all levels—state, congressional, and presidential. Something was needed to arouse public opinion in support of the war. Fort Pillow was used to provide that stimulus.

Post-war, the name of Bedford Forrest came to be associated with the Ku Klux Klan. The assertion that Forrest was head of the Klan has been repeated in so many books as to be beyond counting. The problem with this assertion is that no historian has ever produced any primary source document which proves Forrest held that position. Writers of secondary sources cite each other but none cite a document from the 1860—70's to prove their case. In short, there is no valid historical evidence to support the claim that Forrest was head of the Klan.

Eric Foner is considered by many to be the

leading contemporary historian of the Reconstruction Era. His book, *Reconstruction: America's Unfinished Revolution,* discusses the Klan in great detail over a number of chapters. The name of Bedford Forrest is never mentioned. A growing number of academic historians admit that there is no evidence linking Forrest to the Klan, yet still the folklore is repeated whenever the name of Forrest is mentioned.[83]

The historical fact is that a congressional investigating committee cleared Forrest of any involvement with the Klan and commended him for his opposition to the group. Forrest also became an advocate for African Americans exercising the right to vote. Historians who condemn Forrest for his supposed affiliation with the Klan either ignore these facts or make great efforts to dismiss them but in doing so they violate the duty of an historian to deal with facts and not to substitute personal opinions or folklore for primary sources.

Forrest was a fierce fighter. His force held out until May 9, 1865, a month after the fighting had ended in Virginia and several days after it had ended in North Carolina. Forrest accepted the inevitable with good grace and advised his

---

[83] See Eric Foner, *Reconstruction: America's Unfinished Revolution, 1863-1877* (New York: Harper Perennial, 2014). Originally published, 1988.

men to do likewise. The farewell address he issued to his command at Gainesville, Alabama is a model of calmness and reconciliation.

There were no U.S. forces present to accept the surrender of Forrest's command. On the morning of their departure the men fell in for roll call and Forrest's final order was read aloud. The men then marched by their own ordinance sergeants and turned in their weapons, the artillery was parked in a grove of trees, and the men then reported to their regimental adjutant to received previously printed and signed paroles. Then they went home.

What does Forrest's final address tell us about his ideas concerning the cause of the war? The order states that, for Forrest, the causes of the war were irrelevant but that the result of the war was obvious, the South had lost and the Confederacy was no more. The only thing for sensible people to do was accept the results and get on with their lives. This statement reflects the same pragmatic attitude with which he had fought during the war. It should be noted that Forrest had opposed secession and had voted against it in February 1861 when Tennessee took its first vote on the issue. Forrest stood by the Union as long as the Union stood by the existing laws. Once respect for law was abandoned Forrest moved to protect his home.

Forrest's Escort Company and Staff formed an association even before the United Confederate Veterans were formed and they regularly read aloud the Farewell Address. The sound advice it contained stood them in good stead during the hard economic times that followed the war. The words do much to disprove the common public impression that Forrest was a monster.

Major General George Gordon Meade

Address to the Army of the Potomac, USA

June 28, 1865

Major General George Gordon Meade, photographed by
James Fowler Rusling. Contributing library: LOC.

Headquarters Army of the Potomac,
June 28, 1865.

Soldiers:

This day, two years, I assumed command of you, under the order of the President of the <u>United States</u>. To-day, by virtue of the same authority, this army ceasing to exist, I have to announce my transfer to other duties, and my separation from you.

It is unnecessary to enumerate here all that has occurred in these two eventful years, from the grand and decisive Battle of Gettysburg, the turning point of the war, to the surrender of the Army of Northern Virginia at Appomattox Court House. Suffice it to say that history will do you justice, a grateful country will honor the living, cherish and support the disabled, and sincerely mourn the dead.

In parting from you, your commanding general will ever bear in memory your noble devotion to your country, your patience and cheerfulness under all the privations and sacrifices you have been called upon to endure.

Soldiers! having accomplished the

work set before us, having vindicated the
honor and integrity of our Government
and flag, let us return thanks to Almighty
God for His blessing in granting us victory
and peace; and let us sincerely pray for
strength and light to discharge our duties
as citizens, as we have endeavored to
discharge them as soldiers.

Geo. G. Meade,
Major General, U. S. A.[84]

George Meade was born in Spain, the son of
an American citizen representing the U.S.
Naval Department. He returned to the United
States as an infant and was later given an
appointment to West Point. Meade was a good
student and graduated nineteenth in his class in
1835 but he resigned from the army to pursue a
career in civil engineering. A civilian career
proved to be difficult for Meade and he asked to
be reinstated in the army in 1842 in the Corps of
Topographical Engineers. He served in the
Mexican War but saw no major combat.

---

[84] George G. Meade, *Life & Letters of George Gordon
Meade, Major General--U.S. Army* (New York: Charles
Scribner's Sons, 1913), Vol. 2, 215-16.

Following the war Meade worked designing and constructing lighthouses and breakwaters along the Atlantic coast.

With the outbreak of the War Between the States Meade was given command of a brigade of Pennsylvania volunteers and worked helping design the defenses for Washington, D.C. In the summer of 1862 Meade's command joined the Peninsula Campaign and fought in several engagements there. He was seriously wounded at Glendale but recovered in time to fight at Second Manassas. He did so well he was promoted to command a division. He performed well again at Sharpsburg and was given temporary command of a corps. Following Fredericksburg the command of the Fifth Corps was made permanent and Meade led that unit in the Chancellorsville campaign.

Joseph Hooker resigned only three days before the onset of the Battle of Gettysburg and command of the Army of the Potomac devolved on Meade. A week later Meade could make a claim no other Union general could equal—he had defeated Robert E. Lee.

Gettysburg was not the personal success Meade might have expected. Political scheming in the officer corps of the Army of the Potomac hindered his efforts to exercise command. Lincoln and the Northern press demanded that a pursuit of Lee be mounted immediately following Gettysburg, disregarding the battered condition of Meade's army. The fall season of campaigning resulted in Meade being stymied by Lee at Bristoe Station and at Mine Run.

Part of the criticism of Meade seems to have arisen from his connection with George McClellan. Both men had ties to Philadelphia and with socially prominent Philadelphia families. Both had been conservative Whigs until the mid-1850s when the controversy over slavery destroyed the Whigs. The more liberal Whigs, like Lincoln, became Republicans while the more conservative Whigs supported the Stephen Douglas Democrats. Meade felt his brigadier general's commission "was due to him McClellan, and almost entirely to him."

Meade also agreed with McClellan's view of the goals for the war since McClellan stood for the idea of limiting the war strictly to national reunion, leaving the slavery question out of the picture entirely. He frankly hoped that "the *ultras* on *both* sides" would somehow "be repudiated, & the masses of conservative & moderate men may compromise & settle the difficulty." Meade had a personal interest in compromise because of family ties. Virginia Governor Henry Wise was one of Meade's brothers-in-law on his wife's side, and two of his sisters had married Southerners. His sister Charlotte, in fact, saw her Mississippi plantation pillaged by Union soldiers, and she lost two of her sons fighting for the Confederacy.

The victory Meade desired was a limited one that would either convince the South that "it is useless to contend any longer," or one that induced "the people of the North...to yield the independency of the South on the ground that it does not pay to resist them."[85]

With the arrival of Grant in the east in 1864, Meade became a figurehead and was well aware of it. Grant frequently snubbed Meade by preferring to listen to his own associates from the west who had come east with him and by having Philip Sheridan and William Sherman promoted before Meade, although Meade did receive an earlier date on his commission so as to maintain superior rank over Sheridan.

Meade disagreed with Grant over the tactics of making massive assaults against fortified Confederate positions but when Grant ordered these attacks the men in the ranks saw only that the order to go forward was signed by Meade. Notorious for having a short temper, Meade was not admired by the reporters covering the Army

---

[85] Allen C. Guelzo, "George Meade's Mixed Legacy," *The Cupola*, June 2013, published by Gettysburg College, 40-41.

of the Potomac and was generally mentioned in a negative way in news articles.

In July 1864, Horace Greeley held a peace conference which received a letter from President Lincoln in which Lincoln said that the war could only end when the South abandoned slavery. Lincoln had become wedded to the Emancipation Proclamation's promise but Meade saw the demand as hollow. Meade commented:

> It is a pity Mr. Lincoln employed
> the term "abandonment of
> slavery," as it implies its
> immediate abolition or extinction,
> to which the South will never
> agree; at least, not until our
> military successes have been
> greater than they have hitherto
> been, or than they now seem
> likely to be. Whereas had he said
> the final adjustment of the slavery
> question, leaving the door open to
> gradual emancipation, I really
> believe the South would listen and
> agree to terms. But when a man
> like Horace Greeley declares a
> peace is not so distant or
> improbable as he had thought,
> and when a Republican paper, like

the Times, asserts the people are
yearning for peace, and will not
permit the slavery question to
interpose towards its negotiations,
I think we may conclude we see
the beginning of the end. God
grant it may be so, and that it will
not be long before this terrible war
is brought to a close.[86]

The months following Gettysburg were frustrating for Meade but he continued true to his duty and performed well on most occasions. His temper and his not being allowed to command the Army of the Potomac in his own way prevented him from gaining the love and admiration of his men. He was never the idol of the enlisted man in the way Lee or McClellan were. Written in a stilted and somewhat impersonal tone, it is no surprise that his farewell address is virtually unknown.

In so far as the cause of the war is referred to at all in Meade's farewell address the issue for Meade seems to have been "vindicating the honor and integrity of the country." "Honor," in this context, means Meade saw himself and his

---

[86] Meade, *Life & Letters of George Gordon Meade, Major General--U.S. Army,* Vol. 2, 287.

men preventing the dissolution of the Union, while "integrity" refers to the maintenance of a republican form of government.

As the comments Meade made in regard to the 1864 peace conference show, he favored a gradual end to slavery in a way which would preserve peace. The South, Meade felt, was open to such reasonable terms. Slavery, as a single issue, would not have caused a war if an alternative had been offered which protected the economic interests of the South.

In the years after the war, Meade remained in the Army and spent a good deal of time writing about his service. He died in 1872.

Major General William T. Sherman

Address to the Army of Tennessee and Georgia, USA

May 25, 1865

Maj. Gen. William T. Sherman,
Metropolitan Museum of Art, New York City.

In the Field, Near Washington, D.C.
May 25, 1865
Special Field Orders
No. 76}

The General Commanding announces to the Army of the Tennessee and Georgia that the time has come for us to part. Our work is done, and armed enemies, no longer defy us. Some of you will be retained in service till further Orders.

And now that we are about to separate and mingle with the civil world, it becomes a pleasing duty to recall to mind the situation of national affairs, when but little more than a year ago, we were gathered about the towering cliffs of Lookout Mountain, and all the future was wrapped in doubt and uncertainty, three armies had come together from distant fields, with separate histories, yet bound by one common cause, the Union of our country and the perpetuation of the Government of our inheritance.

There is no need to recall to your memories Tunnel Hill, with Rocky Face Mountain and Buzzard Roost Gap, with the ugly forts of Dalton behind. We were in

earnest, and paused not for danger and
difficulty, but dashed through Snake Creek
Gap and fell on Ressaca [sic], then on to
the Etawah, to Dallas, Kennesaw, and the
heat of summer found us on the banks of
the Chattahoochee, far from home, and
dependent on a single road for supplies.
Again we were not to be held back by any
obstacle, and crossed over fought four
hard battles for the possession of the
Citadel of Atlanta. That was the crisis of
our history. A doubt still clouded our
future, but we solved the problem and
destroyed Atlanta, struck boldly across the
State of Georgia, severed all the main
arteries of life to our enemies, and
Christmas found us at Savannah.

Waiting there only long enough to fill
our wagons, we again began a march,
which for peril, labor, and results, will
compare with any ever made by an
organized army. The floods of the
Savannah, the swamps of the Combahee,
and Edisto, the high hills and rocks of the
Santee, the flat quagmires of the Pedee
(sic) and Cape Fear Rivers, were all passed
in midwinter, with its floods and rains, in
the face of an accumulating enemy, and

Address to the Army of Tennessee and Georgia,
USA

after the battles of Averasboro and
Bentonville, we once more came out of the
Wilderness to meet our friends at
Goldsboro.

Even then we paused only long
enough to get new clothing, to reload our
wagons, and again pushed on to Raleigh
and beyond, until we met our enemy Suing
for peace, instead of War, and offering to
submit to the injured laws of his and our
country. As long as that enemy was
defiant, no mountains, nor rivers, nor
swamps, nor hunger, nor cold, had
checked us, but when he who had fought
us hard and persistently, offered
submission, your General thought it wrong
to pursue him farther, and negotiations
followed, which resulted as you all know in
his surrender. How the operations of this
army have contributed to the final
overthrow of the Confederacy, and the
peace which now draws o'er us, must be
judged by others, not by us, but that you
have done all that men could do has been
admitted by those in authority, and we
have a right to join in the universal joy that
fills our land, because the War is over, and
our Government stands vindicated before

the World, by the joint action of the
Volunteer Armies of the United States. To
such as remain in the Military service,
your General need only remind you that
success in the past was due to hard work
and discipline and that the same work and
discipline are equally important in the
future. To such as go home he would only
say that our favored country is so grand,
so extensive, so diversified, in climate, soil,
and productions, that every man may find
a home, and occupation, suited to his taste,
and none should yield to the natural
impatience sure to result from our past life
of excitement and adventure. You will be
invited to seek new adventure abroad, but
do not yield to the temptation, for it will
lead only to death and disappointment.

Your General now bids you all
farewell, with the full belief that as in War
you have been good soldiers, so in peace,
you will make good Citizens, and if,
unfortunately, new War should arise in our
country, "Sherman's Army" will be the first
to buckle on its old armour and come forth
to defend maintain the Government of our

inheritance and choice.

By Order of / Major Genl. W. T. Sherman
(sgd) L.M. Dayton, AAG.[87]

𝕬t the close of the War Between the States
Sherman was probably the Union commander more hated in the South than any other.
His "March Through Georgia" had, as he put it,
been intended to "make Georgia howl" and that
had been one result. Although not admitted by
most twenty-first century historians, his men
had engaged in depredations, robbery, rape, and
looting. Towns, large and small, had been
burned. Even today the burning of such towns
as Columbia, South Carolina, is attributed by
many historians to Confederates setting fires to
destroy military equipment and the fires spread-
ing unintentionally. Such arguments ignore the
statements of both Union soldiers and Southern
civilians who said the fires were deliberate and
of Union origin.

---

[87] Mark L. Bradley, *This Astounding Close: The Road to
Bennett Place*, 255; *Official Records of the War of the
Rebellion, (O.R.)*, Series 1, Vol. 47, Part 1, 44-46.

Address to the Army of Tennessee and Georgia,
USA

In 1864, in a letter to Secretary of War Edwin Stanton, Sherman gave it as his opinion that there could be no peace "until a certain class of Southerners were all killed." This "class" included women as well as men. Stanton did not contradict this opinion, and soon, subordinates of Sherman, such Major General Robert Milroy, Brigadier General Eleazer Paine, and Major General Stephan Gano Burbage were killing Southern civilians, executing on sight and without trial any who were thought to be involved in leading the opposition to Union occupation.[88]

Sherman saw the cruel policy of total war as the quickest way to end the general suffering caused by the conflict. His policies, at least in his mind, were merciful in that they would end the fighting more quickly than any other.

Prior to beginning the March to the Sea, Sherman met with Mayor James Calhoun and the aldermen of Atlanta to hear a protest against the order to evacuate all civilians from the town, a prelude to burning the place. Sherman told the group:

You cannot qualify war in harsher

---

[88] Sherman to Stanton, June 21, 1864 in *O.R.*, Series 1, Vol. 39, Part 2.

terms than I will . . . We don't want
your Negroes, or your horses, or
your land, or anything you have,
but we do want and will have first
obedience to the laws of the united
States. If it involves the
destruction of your improvements,
we cannot help it. But, my dear
sirs, when peace does come you
may call on me for anything. Then
I will share with you the last
cracker, and watch with you to
shield your homes and families
against every danger.[89]

Note the lower case "u" in united and the
upper case "S" in States. This is the same capi-
talization as used in the Declaration of Independence and in the Treaty of Paris which
ended the Revolutionary War. The language
describes a union of sovereign states. Sherman
was thinking in a way typically associated with
Southerners in emphasizing the rights of states,
even as he negotiated with the aldermen of
Atlanta.

---

[89] Burke Davis, *Sherman's March* (New York: Random
House, 1980), 21; see also 23, 25.

Address to the Army of Tennessee and Georgia,
USA

A softer side of Sherman's personality became clear when he met with General Joseph Johnston at Durham's Station, North Carolina, eight days after Lee had surrendered at Appomattox. Sherman and Johnston met three times to discuss the surrender of not only Johnston's immediate command but also all those remaining in arms east of the Mississippi River. Confederate Postmaster John H. Reagan, present with Johnston, offered a proposal which included the continuation of slavery and which would have returned West Virginia to Virginia as well as making illegitimate the Unionist governments Lincoln has set up in Virginia, Tennessee, and Louisiana. These terms were actually given consideration by Sherman before being rejected by the Andrew Johnston administration.

Quite clearly, for Sherman, the cause of the war was the breakup of the Union. Slavery did not have an important role in Sherman's motivation and he was willing to allow it to continue even after Confederate military defeat. This also reflects his attitude toward African Americans expressed in 1860 when he said the only possible relationship between the races was as master and slave.

This situation will be discussed more fully in

the chapter dealing with Joseph Johnston's farewell address. The terms finally agreed between Sherman and Johnston were identical to those offered the Army of Northern Virginia but with some additional terms which included Confederate naval forces. These naval forces were commanded by Raphael Semmes and consisted of men collected from ships which had been destroyed or disabled and then organized into an infantry brigade. Amnesty for the soldiers and transportation home was also included.[90]

The surrender of Lee's army had been met with rejoicing in the North but Johnston's surrender to Sherman was met with outrage—against Sherman! During the interval between Appomattox and Durham's Station the assassination of Lincoln had taken place and many people in the North saw the act as an act of continuing opposition to, and revenge against, the United States. The public mood had shifted from reconciliation to retribution and the generous terms offered to Johnston's forces were not acceptable to the prevailing opinion.

The old charge that Sherman was insane reappeared in the press. In addition, it was said

---

[90] Bradley, *This Astounding Close,* 216-17.

he was a drunk, a traitor, and a rebel sympathizer. In his position in North Carolina, and isolated by his dislike of reporters, Sherman was unaware of the firestorm until Ulysses Grant showed up, ordered by the secretary of war to go to North Carolina and take command of Union forces there. Sherman went into a rage.

As his army moved north to participate in the grand review planned in Washington, Sherman vented his ire at the government, the press and the public. From his camp outside Washington, Sherman told Grant's adjutant: "Let one newspaper know that the Vandal Sherman is camped near the Canal Bridge where his friends, if any, can find him."[91] To his wife he wrote, "I will never be intimidated by the howling of a set of sneaks. I will take a regiment of my old Division and clear them out."[92] Sherman's men shared his disgust with the situation and were not on their best behavior. Rumors circulated that a military coup was being planned against the government.

The tremendous cheers Sherman received as he led his men down Pennsylvania Avenue

---

[91] Bradley, *This Astounding Close*, 251.
[92] William T. Sherman to his wife, May 8, 1865, Sherman Family Papers, in Bradley, *This Astounding Close*, 171-72.

helped calm his anger and, when he reached the reviewing stand, he made it a point to refuse to shake the hand of Secretary of War Stanton. About a week later Sherman had published his farewell to his officers and men. It is ironic that Sherman, so often depicted as taciturn, produced the longest of any farewell address and that he celebrated the successes of his men more than he emphasized national issues.

General Joseph E. Johnston

*Address to All Confederate Units East of the
Mississippi River, CSA*

April, 1865

**Gen. Joseph E. Johnston,
sometime during the war, U.S. National Archives.**

General Orders No. 22
April 1865

Comrades:

In terminating our official relations, I earnestly exhort you to observe faithfully the terms of pacification agreed upon and discharge the obligations of good and peaceful citizens, as well as you have performed the duties of thorough soldiers in the field. By such a course, you will best secure the comfort of your families and kindred and restore tranquility to our country. You will return to your homes with the admiration of our people, won by the courage and noble devotion you have displayed in this long war. I shall always remember with pride the loyal support and generous confidence you have given me. I now part with you with deep regret—and bid you farewell with feelings of cordial friendship and with earnest wishes that you may have hereafter all the prosperity and happiness to be found in the world.

Joseph E. Johnston[93]

---

[93] *O.R.*, Series 1, Vol. 47, Part 1, 1061.

General Joseph E. Johnston
Address to All Confederate Units East of the
Mississippi River, CSA

Joseph Johnston had a checkered career
during the War Between the States. His
peers and public opinion had high expectations
of him at the beginning of the war. His career in
the pre-war U.S. Army supported such expectations. During the opening phases of the conflict he held a very important position as commander of the troops guarding the line of the
Potomac and, in that capacity, won a major victory in July 1861 along the banks of Bull Run in
the First Battle of Manassas.

The winter of 1861-62 saw overwhelming
forces gather against him, so he took the path of
caution and withdrew his army from the Manassas area to the Peninsula, the area between
the York and James Rivers, where he could
block a U.S. advance toward Richmond.

During the campaigning on the Peninsula,
Johnston displayed what would become his
trademark strategy: fall back and wait for an
opportunity to make a successful counter-attack.
This strategy of delay and retreat worked well
when a large amount of territory was available
but, in the limited confines of the Peninsula,
Confederate leaders increasingly grew nervous
as the sound of Union guns drew closer and
closer to Richmond. The wounding of Johnston

at Seven Pines,[94] and his replacement by Robert
E. Lee, left unanswered what Johnston might
have done if forced back to the final line of fortifications around Richmond—evacuate the capital or fight a desperate battle against superior
numbers.

Recovering from his wounds suffered at
Seven Pines, Johnston served as commander of
a department in the western area of the war,
officially overseeing Braxton Bragg and the
commanders of smaller forces. He was given a
combat assignment in the summer of 1863 and
ordered to gather forces to operate against the
rear of Grant's force besieging Vicksburg but
was never able to gather sufficient manpower to
make his force effective. It was not until 1864
that he returned to combat leadership, replacing
Bragg following the debacle suffered by the
Confederates at Missionary Ridge.

During the Atlanta Campaign of 1864,
Johnston skillfully managed the Army of Tennessee, making very few mistakes and always

---

[94] Johnston was wounded the night of May 31, 1862. The
Battle of Seven Pines, also known as the Battle of Fair
Oaks, or Battle of Fair Oaks Station, took place from
May 31 to June 1, 1862. See
https://www.encyclopediavirginia.org/seven_pines_battle
_of, accessed May 17, 2020.

getting his men in place to block the advance of
Sherman's forces. Outnumbered almost three to
one, it is no surprise that he was forced closer
and closer to Atlanta. It should be noted that the
objective assigned to Sherman was not the capture of Atlanta but the destruction of the Army of
Tennessee. To that extent Johnston was successful in the use of the tactic of delay, retreat,
and look for an opportunity to counter-attack. It
is interesting to speculate what might have
happened if Sherman had captured Atlanta but
the Army of Tennessee had remained strong,
not having suffered high casualties as it did
under the command of John B. Hood. Would
Sherman have dared attempt the March to the
Sea in the face of a strong Confederate army? Or
would the rest of 1864 have been spent in maneuvering against Johnston?

The facts are that Johnston was again removed from command because of doubts about
his strategy, and Hood did take command of the
Army of Tennessee.

The term of Hood's command can be
summed up by a song attributed to survivors of
the Army of Tennessee as they retreated from
Nashville:

Now I am going southward, for my

heart is full of woe.
I'm going back to Georgia to find my
    Uncle Joe.
You may talk about the Yellow Rose and
    sing of Aura Lee
But the "gallant Hood of Texas" has
    played hell in Tennessee.

Johnston did have the "hearts and minds" of his men. Johnston worked hard to provide as much food and equipment as possible. He took care of the lives of his men by not making reckless attacks when maneuver would achieve the same goals, and he let himself be seen among the troops. Even in the final campaign in the spring of 1865, when Johnston swept up the rags and tatters of the Army of Tennessee and all others he could find, the men responded cheerfully and positively to his leadership. With these men Johnston fought what may have been his best planned and executed battle at Bentonville. No matter his ability as a leader or his popularity with the men, Johnston's strategy condemned him in the sight of the Confederate War Department and the administration of Jefferson Davis.

On April 13, 1865 at Greensboro, North Carolina, Jefferson Davis and members of his

cabinet met with Johnston and General P. G. T.
Beauregard to discuss the situation of the country. The two generals advised the civilians that
the military situation was hopeless and that
negotiations should be opened to stop the loss of
life. A letter was drafted by Davis, and sent over
Johnston's signature to Sherman, proposing a
truce which would allow *civil authorities* (emphasis added) to negotiate an end to the war.

On April 17, Sherman and Johnston met at
the home of the Bennett family at Durham Station, North Carolina. At that meeting Johnston
was informed of the assassination of Lincoln.
Sherman and Johnston agreed to the proposal
sent on April 13 and Johnston left to secure
authorization from Davis for the surrender of all
Confederate forces. Sherman agreed, insisting
that Lincoln's first priority had been the preservation of the Union. Johnston inferred that
other topics were open to negotiation, as the
letter from Davis had claimed. Clearly, Sherman
did not see the war as having as its objective the
ending of slavery, as stated earlier.

The April 13 proposal was dictated by Johnston but was heavily influenced by John A.
Reagan. It proposed that existing Southern state
governments would be retained; that the personal, political, and property rights of Southern

people would be preserved under the Constitution; that all Southerners would receive amnesty for wartime acts; and that hostilities be suspended while the civil authorities negotiated.[95]

On April 18, Sherman and Johnston met again and Major General John C. Breckenridge was invited to join the discussion to explain some of the legal points involved. Breckenridge spoke eloquently for five or six minutes when Sherman interrupted: "See here, gentlemen, just who is doing this surrendering, anyhow? If this thing goes on you'll have me sending a letter of apology to Jeff Davis."[96]

Sherman then wrote out his own terms. These proposed an armistice which could be ended by either side with 48 hours notice; the dispersal of Confederate units to their state capitals where they would turn in their arms; recognition of existing Southern state governments provided their officers took the oath of allegiance to the United States; establishing Federal courts in the South; a guarantee of personal, political, and property rights as defined by the U.S. and state constitutions; general amnesty

---

[95] Bradley, *This Astounding Close*, 171-72.
[96] Ibid., 172.

to Southern people; and an immediate cessation
of the war. Johnston gladly accepted these
terms. Although Johnston assumed that slavery
as a legal institution was dead, the terms proposed by Sherman left the question open to
debate. Clearly, neither Johnston nor Sherman
saw slavery as the cause of the war. Nor did
Johnston concern himself with what had caused
the conflict. He was interested in getting the
best terms possible for his men and for the
South.

No wonder that when the official dispatch
from Sherman proposing these terms arrived in
Washington on April 21, a political fire-storm
erupted. Grant was sent to meet with Sherman
and was instructed to declare an end to the truce
(which he did only in a nominal fashion) and to
make sure political issues were not included in
the surrender terms; and that no recognition
was given to Confederate civil authorities.

On April 25, Sherman and Johnston met for
a last time to work out revised terms of surrender. The agreement reached was similar to the
Appomattox terms. Johnston's men were to
cease from all acts of war; Confederate arms and
supplies were to be deposited at Greensboro;
rolls of all men were to be prepared and paroles
given; officers could retain side-arms, horses,

and personal baggage; officers and men were protected by their parole so long as they followed the laws in force. Johnston suggested, and it was agreed, that field transportation would be loaned to the Confederates until they reached their home areas; the units could retain one-seventh of their weapons for protection on the way home; individual soldiers could keep their horses and personal property; troops from the Trans-Mississippi would receive water transportation, as available, from Mobile; paroles were to be signed by the immediate commander of the men; and naval forces with Johnston were included.[97]

Whatever else may be said of his military abilities, Johnston bargained shrewdly and well on behalf of his command when faced with the necessity of surrender. At the farm known as Benton Place near Durham Station, North Carolina, Johnston managed to secure for his command generous terms which protected them from the wave of animosity toward the South which followed the murder of Lincoln. He provided many of them with draft animals to take home to begin farming; he provided them with items (salt, yarn) to barter for food on their way

---

[97] Ibid., 216-17.

home; and those who lived farthest away got help with travel. This was, perhaps, his finest hour as a commanding officer.

The farewell address issued by Johnston was not intended solely for the troops gathered in and around Durham Station. It included all Confederate units east of the Mississippi River since that was the bounds of his command. The order containing Johnston's farewell is dated "April 1865" but has no day since it would be received by different commands at various times. It was actually issued by his headquarters on May 2, 1865.

Johnston was a career military officer although he was out of the army for a short time in the 1830's. He was the highest ranking officer to resign from the United States Army to join the Confederacy. As a career officer, Johnston did not have a large economic investment in slaves. He was not from a plantation family but he did own slaves who acted as personal servants.

It was not uncommon for officers in the U.S. Army also to own slaves, and several continued to own slaves while serving the Union during the war. Johnston's commitment to the South cannot be traced to a commitment to the institution of slavery. His reasons for fighting the war must be sought elsewhere.

Lt.-Col. Charles T. Trowbridge

Address to the 33d United States Colored Troops, USA

February 9, 1866

C. T. TROWBRIDGE
LIEUT. COL. 33D U. S. C. T.

**Lt. Col. Charles T. Trowbridge,
from a Facebook group.**

Charles Tyler Trowbridge
33rd USCT Headquarters
33d United States Colored Troops,
   Late 1st South Carolina Volunteers,
Morris Island, S.C.
February 9, 1866.
General Orders, No. 1.

COMRADES,—The hour is at hand when we must separate forever, and nothing can ever take from us the pride we feel, when we look back upon the history of the First South Carolina Volunteers,—the first black regiment that ever bore arms in defense of freedom on the continent of America.

On the ninth day of May, 1862, at which time there were nearly four millions of your race in a bondage sanctioned by the laws of the land, and protected by our flag,—on that day, in the face of floods of prejudice, that well nigh deluged every avenue to manhood and true liberty, you came forth to do battle for your country and your kindred. For long and weary months without pay, or even the privilege of being recognized as soldiers, you labored on, only to be disbanded and sent to your homes, without even a hope of reward. And when our country, necessitated by the deadly struggle with armed traitors, finally granted you the opportunity again to come forth in defense of the nation's life, the alacrity with which you responded to the call gave abundant evidence of your readiness to strike a manly blow for the liberty of your race. And from that little band of hopeful, trusting, and brave men, who gathered at Camp Saxton, on Port Royal Island, in the fall of 1862, amidst the terrible prejudices that then surrounded us, has grown an army of a hundred and forty thousand black soldiers, whose valor and heroism has won for your race a name which will live as long as the undying pages of history shall endure; and by whose efforts, united with those of the white man, armed rebellion has been conquered, the millions of bondmen have been emancipated, and the fundamental law of the land has been so altered as to remove forever the possibility of human slavery being re-established within the borders of redeemed America. The flag of our fathers, restored to its rightful significance, now floats over every foot of our territory, from

Maine to California, and beholds only freemen! The prejudices which formerly existed against you are well nigh rooted out.

Soldiers, you have done your duty, and acquitted yourselves like men, who, actuated by such ennobling motives, could not fail; and as the result of your fidelity and obedience, you have won your freedom. And O, how great the reward!

It seems fitting to me that the last hours of our existence as a regiment should be passed amidst the unmarked graves of your comrades,—at Fort Wagner. Near you rest the bones of Colonel Shaw, buried by an enemy's hand, in the same grave with his black soldiers, who fell at his side; where, in future, your children's children will come on pilgrimages to do homage to the ashes of those that fell in this glorious struggle.

The flag which was presented to us by the Rev. George B. Cheever and his congregation, of New York City, on the first of January, 1863,—the day when Lincoln's immortal proclamation of freedom was given to the world,—and which you have borne so nobly through the war, is now to be rolled up forever, and deposited in our nation's capital. And while there it shall rest, with the battles in which you have participated inscribed upon its folds, it will be a source of pride to us all to remember that it has never been disgraced by a cowardly faltering in the hour of danger or polluted by a traitor's touch.

Now that you are to lay aside your arms, and return to the peaceful avocations of life, I adjure you, by the associations and history of the past, and the love you bear for your liberties, to harbor no feelings of hatred toward your former masters, but to seek in the paths of honesty, virtue, sobriety, and industry, and by a willing obedience to the laws of the land, to grow up to the full stature of American citizens. The church, the school-house, and the right forever to be free are now secured to you, and every prospect before you is full of hope and encouragement. The nation guarantees to you full protection and justice, and will require from you in return the respect for the laws and orderly deportment which will prove to every one your right to all the privileges of freemen.

Address to the 33d United States Colored Troops, USA

To the officers of the regiment I would say, your toils are ended, your mission is fulfilled, and we separate forever. The fidelity, patience, and patriotism with which you have discharged your duties, to your men and to your country, entitle you to a far higher tribute than any words of thankfulness which I can give you from the bottom of my heart. You will find your reward in the proud conviction that the cause for which you have battled so nobly has been crowned with abundant success.

Officers and soldiers of the Thirty-Third United States Colored Troops, once the First South Carolina Volunteers, I bid you all farewell!

By order of Lt.-Col. C. T. TROWBRIDGE, commanding Regiment
E. W. HYDE, Lieutenant and
Acting Adjutant.[98]

---

[98] Charles Taylor Trowbridge, "Six Months in the Freedmans Bureau with a Colored Regiment," *Papers of the Minnesota Commandery of the Military Order of the Loyal Legion of the United States*, Series 6, Vol. 32, No. 1.

The African American units officially known as United States Colored Troops (USCT) are currently celebrated among many students of the war. The best-known African American unit, among general readers, is the 54th Massachusetts and this fame rests largely on the movie "Glory," released in 1989, which celebrated the unit and its commander, Colonel Robert Gould Shaw. Approximately 180,000 African American men served in the United States armed forces during the War Between the States and most of these troops were recruited in the South since that is where the bulk of the African American population was located.

Not generally known is the fact that not all these men were volunteers who made a bold decision to fight for their freedom. In 1863, when the recruitment of African Americans was approved by the U.S. War Department, several commanders of U.S. forces simply announced that all the black men employed as teamsters, laborers, cooks, and servants to officers were now in the army. The men were not asked, they were told. In refugee camps it was not unusual for all able-bodied African American males to be rounded up and told that if their families were to continue to be allowed to stay in the camps the men must enlist. There were cases of "loyal" slave owners being allowed to bring their slaves to enlist and receiving the enlistment bonus as compensation for the loss of their slaves. There were also cases of U.S. Army officers making strenuous objections to the recruitment of African American soldiers because these commanders depended on the labor of African Americans to support their units. These laborers were not volunteers either. The usual practice was to impress all able bodied black men and put them to work without pay. In short, they became forced labor for the U.S. Army. It is ironic that officers of the U.S. Army went on the record stating that these men were more valuable as laborers than as soldiers, even though their status was no different from that of slaves.

Contemporary historians downplay the role of African Americans who were doing the same things in the service of the Confederacy. The term "camp slave" has been applied to those serving Confederate forces, but the same term is applicable to many of those serving the United States.[99]

---

[99] Michael R. Bradley, *With Blood and Fire: Behind Union Lines in Middle Tennessee, 1863-1865* (Shippensburg, PA: Burd Street Press, 2003), 169-72; Union Provost Marshal Records, File of Individual Citizens, Microfilm Collection, National Archives, Microfilm Roll 285, 151;

Often the USCT were relegated to fatigue details or to guarding supply bases and rail lines far to the rear of the fighting. In some of the major battles where they fought, the Battle of the Crater and the Battle of Nashville for example, the USCT were abominably led and suffered very high losses because of incompetent officers.[100]

Despite poor leadership, on many occasions the enlisted men generally fought bravely. Following the Battle of Nashville it was a Confederate officer who paid the USCT their highest compliment for their bravery in their futile assault on Peach Tree Hill.

The 33rd United States Colored Troops (USCT) was raised in and around Port Royal, South Carolina from the African American population which effectively became free following the occupation of the Sea Islands by United States forces in early 1862. At first this unit was designated the 1st South Carolina Volunteers

---

Rufus B. Saxton, "General Saxton Protests Against the Forced Enlistment of Freed Slaves," *After Slavery: Educator Resources,* accessed June 18, 2018; William A. Dobak, *Freedom by the Sword* (Washington, DC: Center of Military History, U.S. Army, 2011), 265ff.

[100] Trowbridge, "Six Months in the Freedmans Bureau with a Colored Regiment," Series 6, Vol. 32, No. 1.

(African Descent) and was authorized by General David Hunter. Many of the men in this regiment were forced to enlist, causing such disruption in the African American community, that Hunter's action was disavowed by the Lincoln administration and the regiments disbanded. When recruitment of African Americans was approved in 1863, the unit was reorganized as the 33rd USCT under the command of Colonel Thomas Wentworth Higginson.

The regiment fought skirmishes along the Georgia and South Carolina coast, participated in the occupation of Jacksonville, Florida, and again saw service in South Carolina. Colonel Higginson was disabled in early 1864 and the regiment came under the command of Charles Tyler Trowbridge. Under Trowbridge's command they saw service in the final days of the bombardment of Charleston, South Carolina, and then spent a year, February 1865—February 1866, on picket and provost duty.

Trowbridge had enlisted as an orderly under General Hunter but volunteered to command a company in the 1st South Carolina, receiving a promotion to captain. With the organization of the 33rd USCT, Trowbridge was promoted to major, then was made lieutenant colonel when he assumed command of the regiment.

This record of promotion was common among the men who became officers in the USCT. Federal law restricted African Americans to holding no rank higher than sergeant so all commissioned officers in the USCT were white. Men who were not abolitionists scorned the USCT, and service in their ranks was looked down upon by many soldiers. Some of those who were willing to accept command in USCT units were often, like Trowbridge, pre-war abolitionists but did not have the military training or education to become officers in all-white units. By accepting service in the USCT men like Trowbridge were upholding their beliefs as well as forwarding their careers, but the majority of men serving as officers in USCT units were mere opportunists.

The lack of training and experience on the part of the white USCT officers often caused unnecessary casualties, unfortunately, among their men. The inexperience and lack of training sometimes caused these officers to step over the line of military law and conduct both during and after the war.

One such occurrence, not discussed by most historians, took place on June 15, 1864. A brigade of USCT commanded by Colonel Samuel A. Duncan was part of a force led by Major

General William F. Smith, Eighteenth Corps commander, sent to break through the lightly held defenses south and east of Petersburg, Virginia. Duncan led the 4th, 5th, 6th, and 23rd USCT regiments in an attack on part of the Confederate Dimmock Line, designed Battery No. 7 and Battery No. 8.

After a day of marching, maneuvering, and skirmishing, the USCT brigade got into position to attack the Confederate fortifications. Instead of sending in a column of attackers their commander sent forward an increasing cloud of skirmishers. This allowed the attackers to storm the fortifications with a minimum of loss.[101]

Once inside the fortifications discipline broke down and fury took over. "They shouted 'Fort Pillow' and the Rebs were shown no mercy" Private Charles Beman wrote in a letter home.[102]

Beman's observation is substantiated by a reporter for the *New York Tribune* who reported

---

[101] *O.R.* Series 1, Vol. 40, Part 1, pp 705-06, 722; Vol. 51, Part 1, pp 267-68.

[102] Charles T. Vernon to his father, cited in Edwin S. Redkey, ed., *A Grand Army of Black Men: Letters from African-American Soldiers in the Union Army 1861–1865*, Cambridge Studies in American Literature and Culture, Series Number 63, 1992, 99.

a conversation between a staff officer and a sergeant of one of the USCT regiments:

> You had a pretty tough fight there on the left.

> Yes, Sir, and we lost a good many good officers and men.

> How many prisoners did you take, sergeant?

> Not any alive, sir.

The headline for the article in which this conversation is recounted reads "The Assault on Petersburg — Valor of the Colored Troops — They Take No Prisoners and Leave No Wounded."[103]

Colonel Delvan Bates, commanding the 30th USCT wrote to his father: "the colored soldiers fight splendidly. They took no prisoners."[104] Bates would rise to the rank of Brevet

---

[103] "The Assault on Petersburg — Valor of the Colored Troops — They Take No Prisoners and Leave No Wounded," *New York Tribune*, June 24, 1864.
[104] Delvan Bates to his father, June 27, 1864, *Bates Letters*, U.S. Army Center for Military History.

Brigadier General and would command a brigade of USCT.

Chaplin Henry M. Turner, an African American minister serving with the 1st USCT, wrote to a church publication:

> When the attackers got into the
> forts a few Confederates held up
> their hands and pleaded for
> mercy, but our boys thought that
> over Jordan would be the best
> place for them and sent them
> there, with a very few
> exceptions.[105]

Turner would later become a bishop of the African Methodist Episcopal Church.

The Confederate defenders of the positions were Wise's Brigade and the Petersburg Home Guard, which was comprised of old men and boys.[106]

One wonders why this massacre is not as well known as the event at Fort Pillow.

---

[105] *Christian Recorder*, July 9, 1864.
[106] Henry A. Wise, "The Career of Wise's Brigade," *Southern Historical Society Papers*, a 52 volume publication of the Southern Historical Society staring in 1876, Vol. 25, p. 13.

186 Lieutenant-Colonel Charles T. Trowbridge
Address to the 33d United States Colored Troops, USA

In September 1865, Trowbridge, acting as Provost Marshal of Newberry, South Carolina, arrested a Confederate soldier, Calvin Crozier, who was returning to his home in Texas. On the night of September 7 Crozier had come to the defense of a group of white women who felt they were being threatened by several soldiers of the 33rd USCT. In an ensuing fight Crozier slightly wounded one of the soldiers.

Trowbridge had Crozier arrested, charged him with murder, and summarily had him shot. Major General Charles Devens, overall commander of the area, found that the man Crozier was accused of killing was very much alive and had suffered only a slight cut during the fight on September 7. General Devens arrested Trowbridge and court-martialed him on a charge of murder. A friendly court found Trowbridge "not guilty" and Devens filed with the War Department a scathing rebuke of the court and of its decision, labeling Trowbridge's action "a most unjustifiable act."

Such acts, both during and after the war, demonstrate that a truthful recounting of history cannot focus on Fort Pillow and the Battle of the Crater without pointing out that massacres were committed by U.S. troops and that some of these were racially motivated.[107]

Higginson and Trowbridge were both ardent abolitionists and favored ending slavery, but it is noticeable that Trowbridge makes no claim that slavery was the sole cause of the war, for he links rebellion, the end of slavery, and the preservation of the Union under the Constitution as the causes of the war. Also, he openly acknowledges the rampant prejudices directed toward African Americans in the North, admitting that slavery had been accepted both North and South as the *status quo.* His Address also points out that recruitment of African American men to serve in the U.S. Army was a "matter of necessity," not one of conscience or morality.

There is also a note of paternalism in Trowbridge's address. He urged his men to return to their former pursuits, albeit as free men, and are told to obey the laws of the land. Since African Americans were not citizens at the time, it is not clear what other course of action was open to the men.

They would also have to contend with disease and sickness, largely brought about by the army they were a part of. Slaves escaping to Union lines were dirty and sick, often starving,

---

[107] Ibid.

often nearly naked, sometimes barefoot in the middle of freezing cold weather, sometimes with open sores festering with vermin. The Union army crowded them all together which promoted the spread of disease. Shelter, if it existed at all, was grossly inadequate. Jim Downs writes in *Sick from Freedom, African-American Illness and Suffering During the Civil War and Reconstruction* that the War Between the States "produced the largest biological crisis of the nineteenth century, claiming more soldiers' lives and resulting in more casualties than battle or warfare and wreaking havoc on the population of the newly freed."[108]

Disease and high rates of death were caused by "the unsanitary conditions of army camps, polluted waterways, unburied bodies of animals and soldiers, overcrowding, dislocation, and the medical profession's uncertainty about how to respond to the massive epidemics that plagued the South, among other issues." This was more devastating for ex-slaves who "often lacked the basic necessities to survive" such as "clean clothing, adequate shelter, proper food, and

---

[108] Jim Downs, *Sick from Freedom: African-American Illness and Suffering during the Civil War and Reconstruction* (Oxford: Oxford University Press, 2012), 4.

access to medicine."[109] They struggled for years after the war. There was a devastating smallpox epidemic that "claimed the lives of thousands of freed slaves from 1862 to 1868."[110]

Union commanders saw the newly freed as a "distraction from larger military objectives" so they had no real concern for them and often moved them "from one camp to another" with indifference. The poor ex-slaves "frequently begged for scraps of uneaten food, worn-out boots, and unused tents."[111]

These facts were deliberately covered up by the army, Northern journalists and the Federal Government because they did not fit the narrative the North wanted to put forward of happy ex-slaves. Federal Government agents "did not tell the stories of the tens of thousands of emancipated slaves who suffered and died during the Civil War from the explosive outbreak of epidemic disease. The names and experiences of these freedpeople were too politically problematic to be recorded."[112]

Black Union soldiers were treated outrageously by the Federal Government. Their story

---

[109] Ibid.
[110] Downs, *Sick from Freedom*, 15.
[111] Downs, *Sick from Freedom*, 4.
[112] Downs, *Sick from Freedom*, 6.

is still being covered up by a legion of dishonest, incompetent or politicized historians.

The families of black Union soldiers suffered enormously and they could do little about it. The "aggressive recruitment of freedmen first as laborers, then as soldiers in the Union army, left their families without a source of income and support, which inadvertently contributed to many freedpeople becoming sick."[113] Soldiers were promised "their salaries would be sent to their families or their families would be able to reside within the camps that employed them"[114] yet it often did not happen. Women and children, with no money, means, food, shelter or clothing, suffered and died in droves.

This was agonizing to black Union soldiers as noted in 1864 by "A. L. Mitchell, lieutenant colonel in the Union army and superintendent of the Freedmen" who wrote:

> 'The colored soldiers have
> complained most bitterly about
> the way they have been treated, by
> their wives being taken away from
> them and sent they knew not to

---

[113] Downs, *Sick from Freedom*, 25.
[114] Ibid.

what camp or plantation.'[115]

A typical example was "Chattanooga, Tennessee in January of 1865, [when] a military official reported that former enslaved people were 'dying by scores—that sometimes thirty per day die & are carried out by wagon loads, without coffins, and thrown promiscuously, like brutes, into a trench.'"[116] In Helene, Arkansas the "bodies of emancipated slaves were placed in the same carts with carcasses of mules and horses to be buried in the same pit."[117] Collecting dead bodies of former slaves shows that "Northerners, allegedly fighting for the freedom and dignity of those subjected to human bondage, were transporting black people like animals."[118]

In many ways, the farewell address to the

---

[115] A. L. Mitchell to John Eaton, May 31, 1864, in *Extracts from Reports of Superintendents of the Freedmen*, complied by Rev. Joseph Warren, 21, in Downs, *Sick from Freedom,* 24.

[116] Maria R. Mann to Elisa, February 10, 1863, Maria Mann to Miss Peabody, April 19, 1863, *Maria Mann Papers*, LOC, quoted in Louis S. Gerteis, *From Contraband to Freedman: Federal Policy Toward Southern Blacks 1861-1865* (Westport, CT: Greenwood Press, 1973), 121, in Downs, *Sick from Freedom*, 27.

[117] Ibid.

[118] Downs, *Sick from Freedom*, 27.

33rd USCT sums up the failure of the abolitionist cause. African Americans were free but hundreds of thousands had become sick in the process and tens of thousands — perhaps hundreds of thousands — had died. Jim Downs states that "Sickness and disease immediately threatened the lives of the roughly 500,000 freed slaves who had escaped from slavery during the Civil War and later the 3.5 million more who were freed when the Civil War ended."[119]

We already know that the Federal Government, which put forth a fraudulent but happy narrative about the newly freed slaves, did not record or report much of their suffering and death, nor did dishonest Northern journalists. The suffering and death of black people was certainly much higher than we know.

A program of gradual, compensated emancipation such as was used in Washington, DC during the war, and was used by most other nations on earth including the Northern states that had phased out slavery before the war,

---

[119] Downs, *Sick from Freedom*, 21. Also, his Footnote 14 to that statement says: "Howard provides a rough estimate that over a half-million slaves were sick during the Civil War years. See O. O. Howard, *Autobiography of Oliver Otis Howard*, vol. 2 (New York: Baker and Taylor, 1907), 364."

would have ended slavery in a much better way than an unbelievably bloody war that killed almost a million people, wounded another million and destroyed much of the country.

But, politically, before the war, no Northern politician would dare suggest that Northerners spend their hard-earned money to free the slaves in the South, who would then come North and be job competition. It just wasn't going to happen.

So, we had our war with all its death and suffering, followed within a few years by Jim Crow discrimination, which began in the North, spread to the South, and resulted in a century of second class citizenship for African Americans.

Brigadier-General Randall L. Gibson

Address to Gibson's Brigade, CSA

May 8, 1865

Brig.-Gen. Randall Lee Gibson,
http://www.generalsandbrevets.com/sgg/gibson.htm,
photographed by Andrew D. Lytle, Sr.

Headquarters <u>Gibson</u>'s Brigade,
near <u>Meridian, Mississippi</u>,
May 8th, 1865.

Fellow-soldiers:

For more than four years we have
shared together the fortunes of war.
Throughout all the scenes of this eventful
revolution you have been fully tried, and
now retire with the consciousness of
having achieved a character for discipline,
for valor, and for unselfish patriotism, of
which you may be justly proud.

There is nothing in your career to look
back upon with regret. You have always
been in front of the enemy; you have never
feasted in soft places at the rear, nor fought
your battles at comfortable firesides. Your
banners are garlanded with the emblems
of every soldierly virtue; more than twenty
battle-fields have seen them unfurled; they
were never lowered save over the bier of a
comrade.

Forget not the good and true men who
have fallen. No sculptured marble may
perpetuate the memory of their services;
but you will wear their names ever green
in your hearts, and they will be enshrined

forever in the affections of the Southern people, in whose cause they fell.

Comrades! henceforth other duties will devolve upon you. Adversities can only strengthen the ties that bind you to your country, and increase the obligations you owe to her interests and her honor. As soldiers, you have been amongst the bravest and most steadfast; and as citizens, be law-abiding, peaceable, and industriousness.

You have not surrendered, and will never surrender your self-respect and love of country.

You separate not as friends, but brethren, whom common hopes, mutual trials, and equal disasters have made kinsmen.

Hereafter you shall recount to your children with conscious pride the story of these rugged days, and you will always greet a comrade of the old brigade with open arms.

Having commanded a company and regiment in the brigade, I have known many of you from the very beginning of the struggle; have been with you through all its varied fortunes, and offer to each one of you a grateful and affectionate

farewell.
May God bless you.

R. L. Gibson, Brigadier-General,
Commanding.[120]

Randall Gibson is not one of the well-known figures of the war nor is his command one of the celebrated units who created a legend for themselves in combat. Gibson, and the Louisiana Brigade, is an excellent example of a great many veterans who did their duty for four years and who formed a strong bond of brotherhood with those with whom they served.

A native of Kentucky, Gibson grew up in Louisiana where his father had moved the family to get better farm land. Sent to Yale, he graduated in 1853 and returned to Louisiana to study law, taking his law degree from what would later be known as Tulane University. Gibson practiced law and owned a sugar plantation where he was a neighbor of Braxton Bragg. It seems the two did not get along and this clash carried over into the war years.

---

[120] Randall L. Gibson, "Farewell Address to the Louisiana Brigade," *Southern Historical Society Papers* (Richmond: Southern Historical Society, 1917), Vol. 4, 223-4.

When Louisiana left the Union, Gibson volunteered for service, first being an aide to Governor Thomas Moore, then captain in the 1st Louisiana Artillery, and then colonel of the 13th Louisiana. In their first battle, Shiloh, their brigade commander was wounded and Gibson assumed leadership of the brigade. Following the battle Bragg filed a report which disparaged Gibson's conduct and, in a private letter to his wife, accused Gibson of cowardice. All of Gibson's immediate superiors had praised his actions and he spent a good deal of time over the next several months trying to get a court of inquiry so as to clear his name. He never succeeded in getting a formal hearing. He did go on to establish a solid record in combat at Perryville, Stones River, and Chickamauga.

In early 1864 Gibson was promoted to brigadier and took permanent command of what had come to be known in the Army of Tennessee as the Louisiana Brigade. He led his men through the Atlanta Campaign and they came to respect him highly for his acts of courage under fire. Gibson led his men back to Tennessee following Hood, and in the Tennessee Campaign, the brigade proved its dedication to the Confederate cause. Six hundred and sixty men began the march into Tennessee, only two hundred sixty-two reached Corinth, Mississippi, at the close of the movement. The Louisiana Brigade had been less that a regiment in size when they crossed into Tennessee. They were less than a battalion in strength when they reached Mississippi. Even so, the survivors of that campaign were sent to help defend Mobile in January 1865.

Assigned to defend the post of Spanish Fort, Gibson told his men to "fight with the spade" and they dug elaborate defenses to protect themselves from the overwhelming force gathering before them. When the Union attack began the 2,000 men of the Louisiana Brigade fired 54,000 rounds in forty-eight hours—a very respectable volume of fire for the number of soldiers involved. When it was obvious that the attack would overrun their position Gibson, in the middle of the night, evacuated his men through a swamp using a walkway eighteen inches wide.

When General Richard Taylor surrendered the command of which the Louisiana Brigade was a part, Gibson bade his men "goodbye" at Cuba Landing, Alabama.

His words speak eloquently of the bond which had grown up between he and his men and reflect the devotion with which they supported their cause.

Gibson's farewell address tells us nothing, directly, about his perceptions of the cause of the war. It does tell us a good deal about why the soldiers under his command fought. Gibson speaks of their patriotism and devotion to the attempt to establish a separate nation.

It cannot be argued that their desire to create a separate nation was for the purpose of perpetuating slavery since slavery was under no immediate threat in 1860. If perpetuation of slavery had been their goal they needed only to stay in the Union and send to Washington senators and representatives who would oppose any attempt to reverse the Dred Scott decision of the Supreme Court, which had declared that the national government could not take any action to end slavery.

The country, which was the object of their love, was Louisiana, specifically, and the South, generally. The concept of the United States as a single political entity was foreign to the minds of many people of that day. For them, the United States means their state in a voluntary association with the other states. Loving the United States meant loving one's own state first and valuing the union of all the states as a secondary emphasis.

Like other Confederates, the men of the Louisiana Brigade were urged to be good citizens and to obey the laws but Gibson emphasizes that defeat did not mean shame or remorse. The men of the unit were urged to be proud of their record as soldiers, to display their self-respect, and to keep alive the memory of their comrades who died during the war.

For Gibson, and for his men, the cause for which they fought was home and family, state and local community. Simple things, but very important ones.

Gibson, like many other former Confederates, came to view the end of slavery as a positive result of the war. Post-war, Gibson practiced law in New Orleans and became active in politics. He urged African Americans to exercise the right to vote and advocated that they take an active role in politics including seeking and holding elected office.

Brevet Brig. Gen. William Cogswell

Address to the 3rd Brigade, 3rd Division,
20th Army Corps, Army of Georgia, USA

June 9, 1865

Brevet Brig. Gen. William Cogswell,
Brady-Handy Collection, LOC.

Head Quarters, 3rd Brigade, 3d Div.,
20th Army Corps,
Near Washington, D.C.
9th June 1865
General Orders No. 14

Officers and Enlisted Men of the
3rd Brigade 3rd Division 20th Army Corps,
Army of Georgia.

In a few days your organization will be
broken up. Some of you will go to your
homes, and the civil pursuit of life, while
others remain for still further duty in the
West.

Your noble record, the history of the
deeds of valor you have performed, and of
the part you have taken in this "War of the
great Rebellion" now so gloriously ended,
have preceded you to your homes, while
the West knows them already by heart.

Although I have been with you but six
short months, yet, by your valor, by your
patience, by your fortitude, and by your
courtesies I have learned to love and
respect you, and I shall part with you with
sorrow and regret.

No part of my military life has been so

pleasant as that which links its history with yours.

From the earliest of battle fields to the last grand blow at Bentonville [N.C.], your blood has stained, Alas! too many a sod.

Quick, soldierly in camp, patient, willing and obedient on the march, brave in battle, with never an inch of ground lost, participating to an unusual extent and with unsurpassed valor in the last battle of the War – March 19, 1865 – your record will be remembered wherever the "battles of the Potomac" are known or the "Campaign of Sherman" read.

That the pleasures and comforts of home may attend you that go, that additional honor and laurels may await you that remain, that an Almighty and good God may forever lead you in ways of pleasantness and paths of peace, that industry and virtue may crown you with their rewards, that all that good brave men deserve may be yours, that those who remain may shortly be sent to home and friends, and that the blessings of a kind heaven may always be with you wherever you go, is the last best wish of your

Address to the 3rd Brigade, 3rd Division,
20th Army Corps, Army of Georgia, USA

Brigade Commander.

Wm Cogswell
Bvt. Brig Gen Comm[121]

 illiam Cogswell was born in Massachusetts and attended school there before
briefly enrolling at Dartmouth College which he
left for a two year voyage around the world,
working as a common sailor. On his return he
attended Harvard and entered the practice of
law. He also joined a local militia unit. His family
was active in politics and his father was one of
the founders of the Republican Party in Massachusetts.

Cogswell was practicing law in Salem, Massachusetts when he heard that the 6th Massachusetts had been attacked in Baltimore on
April 19, 1861. He immediately began recruiting
men to form a company enlisted for the duration
of the war. He was successful in doing this in
twenty-four hours, making his the first U.S. unit
which enlisted for the duration. This unit be-

---

[121] William Cogswell, "An Eloquent Farewell Address to
His Troops by a Massachusetts General,"
www.SethKaller.com, accessed July 10, 2020.

came Company C, 2nd Massachusetts.

Cogswell saw combat at Cedar Mountain, Sharpsburg (Antietam), and Chancellorsville, where he was wounded. When he recovered he found his regiment had been sent to join the Army of the Cumberland and that he had been promoted to its commander. As a regimental commander Cogswell fought in the Atlanta Campaign and was named Post Commander of Atlanta following the capture of that city.

When the March to the Sea began Cogswell was placed in command of a brigade comprised of 20th Connecticut, 33rd Massachusetts, 55th Ohio, 73rd Ohio, 26th Wisconsin, and 136th New York. He led this brigade until the end of the war and it saw heavy combat at Bentonville.[122]

Following the war Cogswell entered politics and served in the U.S. Congress as a Republican.

Cogswell and his men had as much opportunity to represent the abolitionist point of view as any. Even in the western armies, where abolitionists were few, those present were likely to be found in Ohio regiments. Yet, in his farewell address, Cogswell says nothing at all about slavery. In so much as he addresses the cause of

---

[122] *O.R.*, Series I, Vol. 47, Part 1, 46-55.

the war at all Cogswell refers only to the "great rebellion." He urges his men to take pride in putting down that insurrection and in preserving the Union, but even for the son of the founder of the Republican Party in Massachusetts, slavery was not the issue which led him to fight.

Cogswell seems to have shared the attitude of most other citizens of Massachusetts in viewing African Americans as not equal to white people. Massachusetts had passed laws segregating their public schools early in the existence of the school system and that practice was upheld by the Massachusetts Supreme Court in 1850. Railroad facilities were segregated. Even at the time of Cogswell's death, 1895, Massachusetts still maintained segregated schools although the state legislature had officially outlawed the practice. The following year, 1896, the United States Supreme Court cited the Massachusetts practice of segregation as support for its ruling in *Plessy v. Ferguson,* which allowed racial segregation nationwide. For Cogswell, and for many others, "free" did not mean "equal" so far as African Americans were concerned.

Colonel John Singleton Mosby

*Address to the 43rd Battalion, Virginia Cavalry,
"Mosby's Command," CSA*

April 21, 1865

**Col. John Singleton Mosby, the Gray Ghost,
from the Brady-Handy Collection, LOC.**

Soldiers! I have summoned you to gather for the last time. The vision we have cherished of a free and independent country has vanished and that country is now the spoil of a conqueror. I disband your organization in preference to surrendering it to our enemies. I am now no longer your commander. After an association of more than two eventful years, I part from you with a just pride in the fame of your achievements and grateful recollections of your generous kindness to myself. And now at this moment of bidding you a final adieu, accept the assurance of my unchanging confidence and regard. Farewell![123]

On April 21, 1865, the men of the 43rd Battalion, Virginia Cavalry, better known as "Mosby's Command," assembled at Salem, Virginia and John Singleton Mosby inspected their ranks. Mosby then sat silent as the commander of each company stepped to the front of his men and read the address. The Farewell

---

[123] Mosby's Farewell Address, April 21, 1865, *J. Henley Smith Papers*, Library of Congress.

Address to the 43rd Battalion, Virginia Cavalry,
"Mosby's Command," CSA

Address made by Mosby to his command is one of the most unusual of the entire war because Mosby did not surrender, he just quit fighting.

John Mosby is, perhaps, the best known lower ranking officer of the entire War Between the States. Mosby had a spectacular career as the leader of partisan rangers but he also benefited from having about him some well-educated and literate men who wrote books about him soon after the war, making him a folk-hero in the South and well known in the North. The area of Northern Virginia over which Mosby and his men held sway became known as "Mobsy's Confederacy" and is still so called today by those who study the history of the war.

Mosby was married and had two children when the war began and was practicing law near Bristol, Virginia. He opposed secession and made it clear that he did not favor the practice of slavery, but he enlisted as a private when Virginia seceded. In 1862, the Confederate government authorized the establishment of partisan ranger units to operate behind Union lines as scouts and to carry on irregular warfare. Mosby was authorized to form such a unit in 1863 and it became famous as the 43rd Battalion Virginia Cavalry.

Partisan units did not live in camps but

Address to the 43rd Battalion, Virginia Cavalry,
"Mosby's Command," CSA

scattered themselves among the civilian population, assembling for duty when called on by
the commanding officer. Such units were popu-
lar because they allowed men to remain at home
for most of the time and they also provided a
degree of protection against Union foragers and
marauders. Many Confederate leaders objected
to the formation of partisan units because they
felt these units encouraged their men to desert
the regular forces and to find a legal haven of
service at home. Union officers often regarded
the partisan rangers as bushwhackers, outlaws,
or guerrillas. However, the men and officers of
the partisan units were regularly enrolled in the
Confederate forces and held rank accordingly.
They were not informal guerrilla bands although
they had similarities to modern insurgent or
guerrilla groups.

Mosby's men lived with the local civilian
population, blending with them most of the time.
They were fed and protected by the local population. They assembled only for specific operations. The war they fought was quite personal
since they fought only in small actions and often
at very close range. Since Mosby did not depend
on his unit staying in camps and observing the
usual protocols of army life the Union authorities had a basis for claiming they were guerrillas

Address to the 43rd Battalion, Virginia Cavalry,
"Mosby's Command," CSA

and not protected by the laws of war. Mosby operated in a gray area with points of law and established practice for and against him. This constant tension affected his view of the war and shaped his attitude for the rest of his life. He died in 1916.

The most spectacular raid made by the "Gray Ghost" occurred in March 1863. Mosby led a few men to the vicinity of Fairfax Courthouse, deep within Union lines, and captured Brigadier General Edwin H. Stoughton, bringing the general and three other officers into Confederate lines. Soon his reputation as an outstanding partisan was growing as was the size of his command. Late in 1863, the 43rd Battalion was increased in size to a regiment.

In 1864, as the struggle grew desperate, Mosby's men came to be viewed as outlaws by Union officials and some of them were executed upon capture. Mosby did not hesitate to retaliate in kind and the practice was dropped.

On October 13, 1864, Mosby's command derailed a west bound train on the Baltimore & Ohio Railroad near Martinsburg. Among the spoils captured was a payroll being delivered to troops by two Union officers. The cash amounted to $173,000 and each man on the raid received a share of $2,100. Because he led from the front, Mosby was wounded several times, the last in December 1864 when he was shot in the abdomen, but he survived and was back in operation in two months. Dozens of operations such as these meant Mosby was like a hornet, stinging Union forces, but not able to stop their progress.

The surrender of Robert E. Lee did not mean the surrender of John S. Mosby.

Negotiations were opened between Mosby and Union officers but, on April 21, 1865, Mosby reached his decision. He assembled his men, told them he was no longer their commander, and formally disbanded the unit. It was left up to each soldier whether or not they would surrender. Mosby turned himself in to the Union provost in Lynchburg, Virginia, in mid-June and received a parole.

In his farewell address to his men Mosby says quite clearly that the reason why they fought was to establish an independent nation. Mosby provides a lesson in understanding the reasons men fought as well as giving an example of how history should be understood. In a letter written in 1907 Mosby said:

> Now, while I think of slavery as
> badly as Horace Greeley did I am

> not ashamed that my family were
> slaveholders. It was our
> inheritance—Neither am I
> ashamed that my ancestors were
> pirates and cattle thieves. People
> must be judged by the standard of
> their own age. . .[124]

Many contemporary students of history would do well to heed the words Mosby wrote. In order to understand history it is absolutely essential to understand the standards of the age under consideration. The past cannot be judged by the standards of the present. If that is done, the past will always be wrong because the past is not now. Those of us alive today have been formed and conditioned by the conditions under which we have grown up and matured. Had we lived in the past we would have been quite different people because the conditions which formed us would have been quite different.

Mosby also reflected what most soldiers, South and North, felt. They did not fight for a political cause, they fought for their country. While many "sophisticated" scholars may scoff

---

[124] "John S. Mosby on Slavery as the Cause of the War," www.ThisCruelWar.com, September 13, 2016, accessed July 11, 2018.

at the sentiment, the concept has long been valued by many: "My country, may she always be right, but right or wrong, my country."

Brig. Gen. Francis Barretto Spinola

Address to the Keystone Brigade, USA

May 28, 1865

Hon. Francis B. Spinola.

Portrait of Brig. Gen. Francis B. Spinola after the war
as a U.S. Congressman from NY, Bureau of Engraving
and Printing.

Head Quarters Keystone Brigade
Washington, N.C. May 28, 1865

158th Penn Col. McKibbin
168th Penn Col. Jack
171st Penn Col. Bierer
178th Penn Col. Dyer

I avail myself of saying to the officers and men of the Keystone Brigade that the time has arrived for me to take my leave of you; and, as your term of service will soon expire many of you, I presume, will abandon the scenes and excitement of the battlefield to once again assume your usual pursuits of industry. In parting let me assure you that I maintain an exalted opinion of you both as officers and soldiers; and, in my official capacity, I thank you for the prompt and cheerful manner in which you have performed your arduous and dangerous duties,—and I shall always look back on my association with you as among the pleasantest hours of my life. You were put under my command at a time when you were fresh from your native state and with few exceptions entirely unacquainted with the dangers and toils of

war. You were placed in no "school of
instruction" but were marched directly to
the front where you have remained
performing your duty in a manner which
reflects great credit upon yourself and
great honor on your state.

Your march from Suffolk, Virginia, to
Newbern, North Carolina, has no equal
since the war began except in General
Banks retreat from Winchester—and that
in this important particular– yours was
toward the enemy, his was from it. Your
conduct at Mill Creek and White Oak
River was equal to that of veteran troops.
Your march to Pollocksville for the
purpose of encompassing the enemy at the
Second Battle of Newbern developed your
powers of endurance, and, at once, gave
you a prominent place among the best
troops in the service.

While aboard the transports in front of
the Rebel batteries on the Pamplico River
you were willing and anxious to incur any
risk or endure any danger necessary to
relieve the beleaguered city of
Washington, N.C. and no troops in the
army could have manifest greater
willingness to make any necessary
sacrifice to relieve the garrison and relieve

it from the perils which surrounded it; but authority higher than you or me checked your patriotic desires.

Your conduct at Blounts Creek fully developed your impetuous desire to encounter the enemy and no soldier ever retired from the battlefield after it had been demonstrated that the column could not advance owing to the destruction of the bridges which crossed the stream. Your reconnaissance to "New Hope School House" was all that could have been asked of any troops; it was a success in every particular.

Your march to, and occupation of, Swift Creek Village, with its accompanying sharp skirmishing as you approached the place and drove the Rebels from it in precipitated flight at the dead hour of night, were worthy the "Old Guard" of Napoleon.

Your conduct throughout has been of a character that has placed the brigade in an enviable position: intemperance and immoral practices, as well as vice in its various forms, have been strangers to the officers and soldiers of the Keystone Brigade—instead of participating and indulging in the practices which are so

prevalent and demoralizing among
soldiers, have inevitably been found on the
Sabbath day joining with each other in
prayer and raising your voices in singing
praises to the Great Ruler of all.

No cause can fail, my Countrymen,
when supported by such men as constitute
the Keystone Brigade. You have done your
whole duty to your country, your state, and
to your families in a manner that no man
among you need be ashamed to
acknowledge that he is one of the
Keystone Brigade—while the authorities of
your state can, with pride, point to you as
an emulation for others who are to follow
you in the field!

We are all called upon to make some
sacrifices in times like the present but the
American who would not obey the call of
his Country in her hour of peril is
unworthy of enjoying the benefits and
blessings of a free government which cost
many lives and much treasure to establish.
No army ever suffered like that of
Washington! No men ever bore their
sufferings with less murmuring than the
brave patriots who pledged their lives,
their fortunes, and their sacred honors
that you and I might enjoy civil and

religious liberty. You need go no further than your own home to find the spot that gave shelter to the Father of his Country, together with the eleven thousand famishing patriots who wintered at Valley Forge, to which place they were traced by the blood which oozed from their unshod feet.

At the expiration of your term of service it is fair to presume that many of you, from age and other causes, will not again enter it; but in the name of Liberty and a bleeding country, I not only appeal to the young men of the Brigade to enlist again, but I implore you, in the name of the men who suffered every conceivable hardship and privation in order to show the despots of the world that man is capable of self government, that you will prove yourselves the proud representatives of the patriots of '76 and never quit the field until this diabolical attempt to destroy the government which Washington and his associates gave us, have been ploughed out by the roots.

F. B. Spinola, Brig. Genl.[125]

---

[125] "Farewell Address to the Keystone Brigade," Field

230 Brigadier General Francis Barretto Spinola
Address to the Keystone Brigade, USA

Few students of the War Between the States have ever heard of Francis Barretto Spinola yet he was well known during his lifetime, in part because he was the first Italian American to serve in the U.S. House of Representatives. A native of Long Island, New York, he practiced law prior to the war, and, like many people with immigrant roots, became involved in Democratic politics. A delegate to the 1860 Charleston Democratic Convention, Spinola supported Douglas in the presidential election but raised a full brigade of troops when the war began and was appointed brigadier in recognition of that feat.

A "political general," Spinola reflected the views of the political leaders of his area. On January 11, 1861, while the first wave of secession was sweeping the lower South, the legislature of New York state adopted three resolutions giving their response to the evolving situation. The first resolution declared the state to be "profoundly impressed with the value of the Union and were determined to preserve it unimpaired" because the Union provided "prosperity and happiness on the American People." The second called on Southern states which had

Printed Broadside, www.HCAAuctions.com, accessed June 20, 2018.

not yet seceded not to do so; and the third resolution provided means for the document to be sent to other states.[126]

What did "prosperity and happiness" mean, specifically to New Yorkers? In 1860 the Southern states produced almost four million bales of cotton, much of which would be shipped to Europe via New York City. Cotton merchants in that city took 40% of the European sales price in fees. The prosperity and happiness of New York City depended on cotton and on the slaves who produced that staple. The mayor of New York, Fernando Wood, had suggested, on January 7, 1861, that Manhattan declare itself independent of both the state of New York and of the Union so it could become a free trade zone. Wood, and many other New York businessmen, knew that a low-tariff South would kill the trade in the high-tariff North and these men spoke accordingly.

No wonder that Spinola made no mention of ending slavery as a reason why he fought. The farewell address issued by Spinola has all the markings of a stump speech. He commends his men on performing well in a series of very routine duties which had amounted to no more than

---

[126] Phil Leigh, "New York Replies to Southern Secession," https://civilwarchat.wordpress.com/2018/07/16/new-york-replies-to-southern-secession, July 16, 2018, accessed July 18, 2018.

marching and a few skirmishes, he digresses into history to raise the image of Washington and the Continental Army at Valley Forge, and he includes an appeal for men to reenlist, even though the fighting was over.

The omission of slavery as a part of the cause for which the Keystone Brigade had fought would not have seemed odd to the soldiers from Pennsylvania, however. On January 24, 1861, the legislature of Pennsylvania had issued a series of resolutions on their response to secession. While the first and third of these resolutions declared secession to be illegal, the second addressed slavery. That resolution did not condemn slavery, but instead, asserted that the slave-holding states had a Constitutional right "to the uninterrupted enjoyment of their own domestic institutions."[127]

The Pennsylvania resolutions do not state why preserving the Union was important enough to go to war but it is clear that the ending of slavery was not one of their objectives. The governor of the state, Andrew Curtin, made clear that Pennsylvania did not wish to have a significant population of African Americans

---

[127] 29 Phil Leigh, "Why Pennsylvania Chose Civil War," https://civilwarchat.wordpress.com/2018/07/13/why-pennsylvania-chose-civil-war, July 13, 2018, accessed July 4, 2020.

during or after the war. When Lincoln announced his intention to issue the Emancipation Proclamation the governor sent the president a letter saying no refugee camps for the freedmen would be allowed in Pennsylvania nor would migration be welcome.

While it seems to be the case that "preserving the Union" involved economic issues for at least some leaders of Union states, it is clear that the abolition of slavery was not a part of that issue. The contemporary contention that "slavery caused the civil war" would have seemed odd to the men of New York and of Pennsylvania as the address of General Spinola shows.

General Edmund Kirby Smith

Address to the District of Texas, New Mexico,
and Arizona, CSA

Gen. Edmund Kirby Smith,
photographer unknown, LOC.

Soldiers—The day after I refused the demand of the Federal Government to surrender this department I left Shreveport for Houston. I ordered the Missouri, Arkansas, and Louisiana troops to follow. My purpose was to concentrate the entire strength of the department, await negotiation, and if possible, secure terms alike honorable to soldiers and citizens. Failing in this, I intended to struggle to the last, and with an army united in purpose, firm in resolve, and battling for the right, I believed God would yet give us the victory. I reached here to find the Texas troops disbanded and hastening to their homes. They had forsaken their colors and their commanders, had abandoned the cause for which they were struggling, and appropriated the public property to their personal use.

Soldiers, I am left a commander without an army—a general without troops. You have made your choice. It was unwise and unpatriotic, but it is final. I pray you may not live to regret it. The enemy will now possess your country and dictate his own laws. You have voluntarily destroyed

our organization and thrown away all
means of resistance. Your present duties
are plain. Return to your families. Resume
the occupations of peace. Yield obedience
to the laws. Labor to restore order. Strive,
both by counsel and example, to give
security to life and property. And may God
in his mercy direct you aright, and heal the
wound of our distracted country.

E. Kirby Smith, General[128]

General Smith was not ready to stop fighting. The Trans-Mississippi Department of
the Confederacy held other such men, Jo Shelby
and Jeff Thompson to mention two. The Trans-
Mississippi had seen small-scale, but intensely
bitter war in Missouri and Arkansas but large
battles had not taken place in its territory since
the early days of the war and along the Red
River in 1864. Since much of the territory had
never been invaded by U.S. troops there existed

---

[128] *Galveston Tri-Weekly News*, June 5, 1865, in Joseph
H. Parks, *General Edmund Kirby Smith, C.S.A.* (Baton
Rouge: LSU Press, 1954), 475-76.

a considerable amount of intact resources for carrying on the conflict. Lacking was manpower. The Trans-Mississippi Department contained about 16,000 soldiers and they knew, even if some of their generals did not, that the war was lost. Most of these men saw what was happening east of the Mississippi and took the initiative to end the war on their own. So, on May 30, 1865, when E. Kirby Smith issued his rather bitter farewell, he was indeed a "general without troops."

Smith's chagrin at the behavior of soldiers in his department can be measured by the tone of the order he had issued only one week earlier:

Headquarters District of Texas,
New Mexico, and Arizona
Houston, April 23, 1865
General Orders No. 20

The major-general commanding
the District of Texas, New Mexico,
and Arizona deems it proper, in
view of recent events, to call upon
the army and patriotic citizens of
Texas to set an example of
devotion, bravery, and patriotism,

worthy of the holy cause of liberty
and Independence, and of the
great efforts heretofore made by
the army and the people of Texas
to advocate and uphold it. The
enemy threatens our coast and
will bring his great and undivided
resources for a successful invasion
of the State. Let him be met with
unanimity and Spartan courage,
and he will be unsuccessful, as he
has been in Texas. Let him be met
at the water's edge, and let him
pay dearly for every inch of
territory he may acquire. Six
hundred Frenchmen under the
First Napoleon recaptured France
from her enemies. Forty-two Irish
soldiers, on our own soil, drove
15,000 men to sea. The Army of
the Trans-Mississippi Department
is larger and in finer order, and
better supplied than ever. There
are no navigable streams in Texas,
therefore the enemy will be
divested of the great power of
steam, which he has elsewhere
relied upon. Crops have been

bountiful; our armies can therefore be supplied in almost any part of Texas. There is no reason of despondency, and if the people of Texas will it, they can successfully defend their territory for an indefinite period. The major-general commanding therefore exhorts the soldiers of the army to stand firmly by their colors, and obey the orders of their officers and recommends to the citizens that they devote themselves still more fully to the cultivation of breadstuffs; for should our armies be unsuccessful in the east, every gallant soldier will rally to the banner of the Confederacy, which will still float defiantly west of the Mississippi River.[129]

Edmund Kirby Smith (the family did not add the hyphen to connect Kirby and Smith until after the war) was a professional military officer, graduating from West Point in 1845 and serving in the war with Mexico and then on the western

---

[129] *O.R.*, Series I, Vol. 48, Part 2, 1284-85.

frontier. Much of his family resided in Florida, although they maintained strong ties with family in New England, and Smith decided to follow his state when Florida left the Union.

As a brigadier general Smith played an important role in the Southern victory at First Manassas and was severely wounded in the battle. Promoted to major-general, he was placed in charge of a military district in East Tennessee, guarding a vital rail link between Virginia and Tennessee and points south.

In the autumn of 1862, Smith moved into Kentucky in coordination with Braxton Bragg although Smith was not under the command of Bragg. During the advance into the Bluegrass State the troops under Smith won a significant victory at Richmond, Kentucky. Promoted to lieutenant general, Smith was sent to command the Department of the Trans-Mississippi, a post he held from late 1862 until the end of the war.

The Trans-Mississippi was the place to which the Confederacy banished officers who failed to measure up to the expectations of the Davis administration or of the army commanders in the East. Smith did not have any personal connections with the Confederate forces in Virginia and, since his home state could not be expected to furnish many men for those forces, his transfer to Tennessee is not surprising. During the Kentucky Campaign of 1862 Smith's failure to cooperate closely with Bragg resulted in much of the blame for the failure of that campaign being placed on him. In truth, Jefferson Davis bears much of the blame for the failure in Kentucky since it was he who created the situation of divided command. But, once Bragg voiced his complaints of Smith to Davis, Smith was on his way across the Mississippi.

Smith spent much of his time as commander of the Trans-Mississippi dealing with administrative duties, trying to cobble together adequate forces to defend the huge region for which he was responsible, and trying to keep open a trade route to Mexico where cotton could be exchanged for European manufactured goods. The brightest day, militarily, for the Trans-Mississippi was the defeat of U.S. general Nathan Banks in the Red River Campaign of 1864. The commander on the ground who secured the victory was Richard Taylor. Smith did not play an active part in the fighting.

In the final days of the war Smith met with governors of the states in his area of command as well as with his leading generals. Many of the military men recognized that the war was lost but a few wanted to carry on the conflict as did the governors.

On May 18, following these meetings, Smith moved his headquarters from Shreveport to Houston. As soon as he was gone from Shreveport the forces left behind began surrendering. By the time Smith reached Houston he learned he was "a general without an army."

Perhaps it was his lack of combat experience which made Smith so certain he could continue the war in Texas. The department he led in the final days of the conflict was devoid of manufacturing capacity so all arms and ammunition would have to have been imported and the only source of money was a trade in cotton with Mexico.

But his dedication to the Confederate cause cannot be questioned. Smith was not a member of the plantation aristocracy and had no personal or family stake in slaveholding. When his address of May 23 speaks of liberty and independence, the precise meaning of the terms are not defined, but his letter of May 30 makes it clear that Smith desperately wanted an independent Southern nation.

Brevet Colonel J. K. Robison

Address to the 16th Pennsylvania Cavalry, USA

June 14, 1865

Brevet Col. J. K. Robison,
picture from Pennsylvania State Senate online.

Headquarters
Sixteenth Pennsylvania Cavalry,
Lynchburg, Va.
14 June 1865

Officers and Men of the Sixteenth
Pennsylvania Cavalry:—The time has come
for us to part; our work is done; an armed
enemy no longer remains to defy us; all
our long fatiguing marches and hard
fighting, and watching for the enemy by
night and day are past; the glorious Stars
and Stripes now proudly wave in all the
States of the old Union. For two years I
have had the honor of being your
commander, and I would not be doing
myself or you justice, without giving
expression to my feelings. Many thanks
are due to both officers and men for their
prompt obedience to all my orders and my
pride in you is ever increased, by the
remembrance of your bravery and
gallantry, as displayed on many bloody
battle-fields, where by your side many a
brave man fell.

The thought that the great Rebellion is
ended is glorious; we do not realize it in its
full purport; you who are about to leave us,

may, as you are about to return to your
homes, families, and friends, who have
been eagerly watching and patiently
waiting this many a day to welcome you
again into the dear home circle. Although I
imagine you will be the more happy for
getting to your homes, and becoming
freed from military restraints, yet I am
sorry to part with you; the endearments
that existed between us is strong, and I
have every reason to believe is mutual.
You have stood by me and our once
beautiful, but now tattered colors, through
many campaigns.

When many things looked dark and
gloomy, you were cheerful. When orders
were strict and exacting, you did not
complain, and when fighting against odds,
overwhelmed by superior numbers, and
compelled to retreat, you evidenced that
praiseworthy characteristic of a good
soldier, repulsed but not whipped, defeated
but not conquered; and when, after many
victorious engagements, the final struggle
came, which proved such a complete
victory to our arms and cause, you
rejoiced not so much over the conquered
foe, as over the crushing of that cause
which threatened the existence of our

beloved republic. And now that we part, I feel sad and gloomy at the thought that I may never again see many of my "brave boys." You are about to return to your homes and firesides to lead the lives of citizens. Let me request, even urge, that you be as good citizens as you have been good, brave and exemplary soldiers.

If any of you have acquired bad habits in camp life, resolve to break off at once, and show to all the world that a good soldier can be a good citizen. You may well be proud of the honors you have won while fighting for the perpetuation of the glorious Union, "the land of the free and the home of the brave." I am sorry we cannot all go home together, but it is ordered otherwise, and it is the duty of every true soldier to obey cheerfully.

I now bid you good-bye. May the kind Providence that has protected us thus far still shield us, and keep us, and prepare us for usefulness in this and a final happy home in a better world.

Yours Truly, (signed)

J.K. Robison, Brevet Colonel
Sixteenth Pennsylvania Cavalry

Samuel E. Cormany, Adjutant[130]

𝕿he 16th Pennsylvania Cavalry was a veteran regiment having served with the Army of the Potomac since late 1862. It was organized under the command of Colonel John Gregg and saw its first active service along the Rappahannock River in January 1863. From that point on, the regiment was involved in all the major campaigns and battles of the Army of the Potomac. The regiment fought in the cavalry engagements which led up to the Battle of Chancellorsville, saw service at Kelly's Ford and Brandy Station before marching to Gettysburg. The troopers had been part of the pursuit of the Army of Northern Virginia and then had been active during the interval between Gettysburg and the Mine Run Campaign.

As 1864 opened, the 16th rode with Kilpatrick on his raid against Richmond and then were part of the Overland Campaign. They guarded

---

[130] Norman Gasbarro, *16th Pennsylvania Cavalry - Farewell Address*, "An address by Brevet Colonel J. K. Robison, of the 16th Pennsylvania Cavalry", http://civilwar.gratzpa.org/2011/07/16th-pennsylvania-cavalry-farewell-address/, July 27, 2011, accessed July 6, 2020.

the Union right during the siege of Petersburg for much of the summer of 1864 but were ordered back north of the James River to support a move Grant made in that direction in August. They remained on active duty throughout the autumn and winter of 1864-65 and were engaged at Five Forks. Pursuing the Army of Northern Virginia to Appomattox, the regiment was then ordered towards Danville and Lynchburg, Virginia. The last of the men were not discharged until August, 1865. During the course of the conflict the regiment lost 105 men killed or mortally wounded and 197 to disease.

The 16th Pennsylvania could claim as good a record as any cavalry regiment, and a better one than most in the Army of the Potomac. They had fought as hard as anyone and they seemed to know for what cause they had fought.

Colonel Robison, in his farewell address, follows a familiar pattern in congratulating his men on their bravery and conduct as good soldiers. The cause for which they had fought was to end the rebellion and to restore the Union, as Robison states in plain language. He also alluded to a desire for reconciliation between North and South when he says the regiment took no pleasure in gloating over a defeated foe but they did rejoice in crushing the threat to the Union. Modern historians argue that the "era of Reconciliation" did not develop until well after the war, at least until a decade had passed. Robison says otherwise. He and his Pennsylvania veterans were ready for the sections to reconcile as soon as possible and to do so as one nation.

There is no mention of slavery as a cause for the war and no hint that ending slavery was the motivation leading the 16th Pennsylvania to enlist and to fight for three years. Restoring and preserving the Union were the issues which led these men to the battlefield.

Why did these men of the Keystone State want so desperately to preserve the Union? Their motivation may be found in every Northern newspaper as the Cotton States seceded, such as this one in *The Philadelphia Press* in January 1861: "It is the enforcement of the revenue laws [tariffs, etc.], not the coercion of South Carolina that is the question of the hour. If those laws cannot be enforced, the Union is clearly gone."[131]

Despite the denials of some ill-informed historians, economic issues, including the desire of Northern manufacturers and business leaders for high tariffs, were huge issues. Northerners

---

[131] Phil Leigh, "Why Pennsylvania Chose Civil War," https://civilwarchat.wordpress.com/2018/07/13/why-pennsylvania-chose-civil-war, July 13, 2018, accessed July 6, 2020.

demanded high tariffs and protection while Southerners made them unconstitutional. Southerners were determined to escape the North's economic control of the South. Taxes had also been huge in the Revolution.

"Preserving the Union" meant preserving the North's cash cow, the source of most of the North's wealth and power.

Major General Henry Warner Slocum

Address to the Army of Georgia, USA

Maj. Gen. Henry Warner Slocum,
Brady Nat. Photo. Art Gallery, LOC.

HQ Army of Georgia
Washington, D.C. June 6, 1865
General Orders #15

    With the separation of troops
composing this army, in compliance with
recent orders, the organization known as
the Army of Georgia will virtually cease to
exist. Many of you will at once return to
your homes. No one now serving as a
volunteer will probably be retained in the
service against his will but a short time
longer. All will be permitted to return and
receive the rewards due them as gallant
defenders of their country. While I cannot
suppress a feeling of sadness at parting
with you I congratulate you on the grand
results achieved by your valor, fidelity, and
patriotism. No generation has ever done
more for the permanent establishment of a
just and liberal form of government, more
for the honor of their nation, than has been
done in the last four years by the armies of
the United States and the patriotic people
at home who have poured out their wealth
with a liberality never before witnessed in
any country. Do not forget the parting
advice of that great chieftain [Sherman]

who led you through your recent brilliant
campaigns: "As in war you have been good
soldiers, so in peace be good citizens."
Should you ever desire to resume the
honored profession you are about to leave,
do not forget that this profession is
honorable only when followed in
obedience to orders of the constitutional
authority of your government. With
feelings of deep gratitude to each and all of
you for your uniform soldierly conduct, for
the patience and fortitude with which you
have borne all the hardships it has been
necessary to impose upon you, and for the
unflinching resolution with which you
have sustained the holy cause in which we
have been engaged, I bid you farewell.

H.W. Slocum
Maj. Gen.[132]

ℌenry W. Slocum was a native of New York
and a member of the West Point class of

---

[132] Charles Elihu Slocum, *The Life and Services of Major General Henry Warner Slocum* (Toledo: Slocum Publishing Co., 1913), 321.

1852. He served in the Seminole War and spent time as part of the garrison of the various military installations at Charleston, South Carolina. He left the army in 1856 and became a lawyer in Syracuse, New York. When the War Between the States broke out Slocum became colonel of the 27th New York Infantry.

The opening battle of the war at Manassas gave Slocum his first combat experience and his first wound. On recovery, he was made commander of a brigade and soon rose to command a division. When he was promoted to major general, he was the next-to-youngest officer of that rank in the service of the United States. Following service in the Peninsula Campaign, Second Manassas, and Sharpsburg, Slocum was given command of the 12th Corps. This command was not engaged at Fredericksburg but saw fierce combat at Chancellorsville.

Slocum became disgusted with the leadership of General Joseph Hooker and was one of the critics who helped convince Lincoln to replace Hooker with Meade. At Gettysburg the 12th Corps held the right of the Union line, a critical position which was heavily attacked by the Confederates. In the fall of 1863, following the battle of Chickamauga, Union forces under the command of Hooker were sent to assist in relieving the Army of the Cumberland at Chattanooga. Slocum's Corps was part of this force but he managed to secure a post guarding the Nashville & Chattanooga Railroad so as not to be under the direct command of Hooker. Later, Slocum was moved to Vicksburg, a relative backwater.

When the Atlanta Campaign began, the 20th Corps was commanded by Hooker but he resigned in July and Slocum was brought from Vicksburg to take command. As part of Sherman's force, he fought in Georgia and the Carolinas.

Although a Republican when the war began Slocum changed parties immediately after the fighting ended and became a Democrat. He served three terms in the U.S. Congress and held numerous offices in the city government in New York City.

In his farewell address, Slocum sounds familiar themes, congratulating his men on their bravery and soldierly conduct. Allusions to the cause for which they fought are somewhat muted, although there is an echo of the Gettysburg Address where Lincoln used the phrase "whether this nation, or any nation so conceived and dedicated, can long endure." Slocum speaks of the government as now being permanently established, implying that the question of secession is settled. The preservation of the Union, for all time, seems to have been the issue uppermost in Slocum's mind and that of his soldiers.

Major General Joseph Wheeler

Address to the Cavalry Corps, CSA

April 29, 1865

Maj. Gen. Joseph Wheeler,
Prints and Photographs Div., LOC.

Headquarters Cavalry Corps
April 29, 1865

GALLANT COMRADES:—You have
fought your fight; your task is done.

During a four years struggle for
liberty you have exhibited courage,
fortitude, and devotion. You are the sole
survivors of more than two hundred
severely contested fields; you have
participated in more than a thousand
successful conflicts of arms. You are
heroes, veterans, patriots. The bones of
your comrades mark battlefields upon the
soil of Kentucky, Tennessee, Virginia,
North Carolina, South Carolina, Georgia,
Alabama, and Mississippi. You have done
all that human exertion could accomplish.

In bidding you adieu, I desire to tender
my thanks for your gallantry in battle, your
fortitude under suffering, and your
devotion at all times to the holy cause you
have done so much to maintain. I desire
also to express my gratitude for the kind
feeling you have seen fit to extend toward
myself and to invoke on you the blessing of
our heavenly Father, to whom we must
always look in the hour of distress.

Brethren in the cause of freedom,
comrades in arms, I bid you farewell.

J. Wheeler, Major General[133]

𝕵oseph Wheeler spent most of his life in the
north, yet chose to serve the Confederacy.
Wheeler's father was a physician from Connecticut who moved to Augusta, Georgia where
Wheeler was born. Before he was in his teens
Wheeler moved back to Connecticut to live with
relatives and completed his schooling there. He
entered West Point in 1854 and though residing
in Connecticut was appointed from Georgia. As a
matter of interest, Wheeler was not a slave
owner, hardly surprising for the son of a Connecticut Yankee who was raised in New England
and who lived on the pay of a second lieutenant
in the U.S. Army.

Wheeler graduated near the bottom of his
class in 1858, attended the Cavalry School at
Carlisle, Pennsylvania, and was sent to the frontier. He was a second lieutenant when the war
broke out but resigned to come south and was

---

[133] Florence, Alabama *Times*, "Wheeler's Farewell
Address," September 21, 1900.

made commander of the 19th Alabama Infantry. The 19th Alabama fought at Shiloh and led a brigade in the fighting around Corinth in the spring of 1862. In October, Wheeler transferred to the cavalry in time to lead Bragg's mounted force in the Kentucky Campaign.

Wheeler performed well in Kentucky and at Stones River where he circled the Army of the Cumberland repeatedly, destroying large numbers of wagons and taking hundreds of prisoners. Following Chickamauga, Wheeler made a raid into Middle Tennessee in an attempt to hamper the Union effort to supply the troops trapped at Chattanooga but this attempt was a failure, indeed, it was close to a disaster.

Wheeler's high point of the war came during the Atlanta Campaign when he defeated a two-pronged Union cavalry raid against the railroads supplying the Army of Tennessee. During this raid Wheeler mangled the Union cavalry and captured Major General George Stoneman, the commander of the U.S. troops.

Wheeler's cavalry corps offered what opposition they could to Sherman's "March to the Sea" and continued to serve in the closing campaign in the Carolinas. After the war, Wheeler engaged in agriculture at a farm called Pond Springs near Courtland, Alabama, was elected to the U.S. House of Representatives, and returned to military duty during the Spanish-American War and in the Philippines, receiving the rank of brigadier in the regular army.

In his farewell address, Wheeler mentions "freedom" and "liberty" as the goals for which he and his men had fought. These ideals are often set forth by Confederates, during and after the war. In the minds of many of these men they were following the path blazed by their grandfathers in the War for Independence against Great Britain.

It is no accident that Jefferson Davis was inaugurated president of the Confederacy on Washington's birthday, that the Great Seal of the Confederacy displays an equestrian statue of Washington or that the first national flag of the Confederacy was alternating red and white stripes with a circle of stars on a blue union. These images of the Revolution captured the issues in the minds of the people who supported the Confederacy. Just as their forefathers had rebelled against a government which was too strong, too intrusive in local affairs, and too remote, so did they. For Confederates like Wheeler, the war was the second war for independence: the War for Southern Independence.

When the attempt at independence failed, Wheeler became one of many former Confederates who dedicated the remainder of their lives to restoring the unity of the nation and serving their country. Because of his service in Cuba and in the Philippines, Wheeler is among the small number of Confederates buried in the national cemetery part of Arlington. There are over 3,000 Confederates who died as POWs buried at Arlington, interred there before the National Cemetery Act was passed.

Soldiers of the 111th Ohio

We are about to separate as soldiers and go to our homes as citizens. Before we part allow me to thank you for the generous courtesy you have always shown me as your commanding officer. The work which we enlisted to perform has been well done, and you go to your homes with the proud assurance of having participated in the most decisive battles of the war. For your heroic conduct at Franklin you were complimented in "General Orders," and on twenty battle fields you have carried the tattered flag of the 111th Ohio in the front line, and sustained it triumphantly. I do not part with men with whom I have been so intimately associated for three long years without feelings of regret. The soldier friendships, formed in the bivouac and on battle field will never be forgotten and I will ever remember your unswerving fidelity with the liveliest emotions of pleasure. You go to your homes as American citizens, knowing what it has cost to maintain our national integrity. Show by upright, honorable lives, my fellow soldiers, that you fully appreciate those sacrifices. Remember our brave comrades who fell at Stone River, Huff's Ferry, Louden Creek, Campbell's Station, Knoxville, Strawberry Plains, Rocky Face, Resaca, Dallas, Burnt Hickory, Pine Mountain, Kennesaw, Peach Tree Creek, Atlanta,, Utoy's Creek, Lovejoy's Station, Columbia, Franklin, Nashvile and Fort Anderson. Many of them are lying in unknown graves. Let us ever cherish their memory with reverence. Let us show by our lives that we fully appreciate the sacrifices of our brave comrades and extend our sympathy and our charity to the soldier's widow and the dead soldier's friend.

Brave comrades, farewell: may Almighty God bless you; and may a grateful people reward you for your many and daring sacrifices for Country, Liberty, and Peace.

Isaac R Sherwood
Lt. Col. & Brevet Brig. Gen. Comm'd'g[134]

---

[134] Ohio History Center, *Farewell Address of Isaac Sherwood to the 111th Ohio Infantry,* June 27, 1865, Box 55, Catalog #4556.

𝕴 saac R. Sherwood was a native of New York but moved with his family to Ohio and attended Antioch college. He became a newspaper editor and then was elected a county judge. Sherwood resigned this position in 1861 to enlist in the 111th Ohio Infantry, first serving as adjutant of the regiment and later rising to the rank of lieutenant colonel commanding the unit. The 111th saw service in Tennessee during the Knoxville Campaign of 1863, fought in the Atlanta Campaign, and was part of the U.S. force sent to Tennessee when Sherman began his "March to the Sea" and Hood moved north.

At Franklin, the 111th Ohio was in the very center of the battle, holding a position near the Carter House and the Cotton Gin, and its performance was such that it was recognized in "General Orders" as Sherwood noted in his farewell address. Following Franklin, the Buckeyes were sent to the Carolinas and were involved in the pursuit of Jefferson Davis and the remnants of the Confederate government. Sherwood was made a brevet brigadier of volunteers in February 1865.

Following the war Sherwood was active in Union veterans affairs, edited several newspapers including the *Toledo Daily Commercial* and the *Cleveland Leader*. He was also active in politics, holding state office as a Republican, then supporting the Greenback Party, and finally switching to the Democrats. Sherwood served in the U.S. House of Representatives from 1906 to 1920. He was defeated for reelection in 1920 largely because he opposed U.S. entry into World War I, declaring he had become a pacifist.

The farewell address Sherwood issued to the men with whom he had so long been associated follows a pattern observable in many of these addresses: there are a series of congratulations on the bravery and fortitude shown, wishes for the future, and some mention of their motives in going to war. Sherwood emphasized that he and his men had served for the purpose of maintaining national unity. Preserving the Union was their motivation. In the final paragraph there appears the word "liberty" but it is used in the typical nineteenth century context of preserving the United States as an independent nation. There is no hint that "liberty" was related to the end of slavery.

Major General Robert F. Hoke

Address to Hoke's Division, CSA

Maj. Gen. Robert Frederick Hoke,
unknown photographer and date, from
http://www.generalsandbrevets.com/sgh/hoke.htm.

Soldiers of my Division:

On the eve of a long, perhaps final separation, I desire to address to you the last sad words of parting. The fortunes of war have turned the scales against us. The proud banners which you have waved so gloriously on many a field are to be furled at last; but they are not disgraced. My comrades, your indomitable courage, your heroic fortitude, your patience under suffering have surrounded these with a halo which future years cannot dim. History will bear witness to your valor and succeeding generations will point with admiration to your grand struggle for constitutional freedom. Soldiers, your past is full of glory. Treasure it in your hearts. Remember each gory battlefield, each day of victory, each bleeding comrade. Think then of your future.

> Freedom's Battle once begun,
> Bequeathed from bleeding sire to son,
> Though baffled is oft, is ever won.

You have yielded to overwhelming forces, not to superior valor; you are

279

paroled prisoners, not slaves; the love of liberty, which led you in the contest still burns as brightly in your hearts as ever, cherish it, nourish it, Associate it with the history of the past. Transmit it to your children, teach them the rights of freemen and teach them to maintain them; teach them that the proudest day in all your proud career was that on which you enlisted as a Southern soldier, entering that holy brotherhood whose ties are now sealed in the blood of your compatriots, who have fallen and whose history is covered with the brilliant records of the past four years.

Soldiers, amid the imperishable laurels that now surmount your brows, no brighter leaf adorns you than your late connection with the Army of Northern Virginia. The star that shone with the splendor over its oft repeated field of victory, over the two deadly struggles at Manassas Plains, Richmond, Chancellorsville, and Fredericksburg has sent its rays and been reflected wherever true courage is admired and wherever freedom has a friend. That star has set in blood, but yet in glory. That army is now of the past. Its banners trail, but not with ignominy; no stain blots its escutcheon, no blood can tinge your face as you proudly announce that you have a part in the past history of the Army of Northern Virginia.

My comrades, we have borne together the same hardships, we have braved the same dangers, we have rejoiced over the same victory; your trials and your patience have excited sympathy and admiration and I have borne willing witness to your bravery. It is with a heart full of grateful emotion for your service and ready obedience that I take leave of you.

May the future of every one of you be as happy as your past career has been brilliant and no cloud ever dim the brightness of your fame. The past looms before me in its illuminated grandeur. Its memories are a part of the past life of each of you; but it's all over now. The sad, dark veil of defeat is between us and a life time of sorrow is our only heritage. You carry to your home the heartfelt wishes of your General for your prosperity.

My command, farewell!

R. F. Hoke, Major General
Headquarters Hoke's Division,

near Greensboro, N.C.[135]

Robert Hoke was justifiably proud of his men, given their record of combat in both the Army of Northern Virginia and in North Carolina. Hoke was the son of a prominent family with a long history of public service to the Old North State. Although not a fiery supporter of secession, he had enlisted in the early days of the war and had risen in rank when his regiment was called to Richmond to participate in the Seven Days battles. From the first his unit made a record as hard fighters. By May 1863 Hoke had been made a brigadier.

The fighting around Fredericksburg in the last hours of the Battle of Chancellorsville almost brought an end to Hoke's military career with a serious wound which kept him out of active service for the rest of the year. On recovering, Hoke was placed in temporary command of a small force charged with restoring order to parts of western and central North Carolina where deserters and outlaws had created a

---

[135] Chip Stokes, "Company B, North Carolina 71st Infantry Regiment....", http://blueandgrayancestors. blogspot.com/2013/05/company-b-north-carolina-2nd-junior.html, May 20, 2013, accessed 7-10-20.

haven for themselves. He handled this difficult chore in such a way as not only to restore order but to rebuild support for the Confederacy. Later in 1864 Hoke exercised independent command of a force which retook Plymouth and Washington, North Carolina, from the Union forces which occupied them since 1862.

Hoke returned to Virginia just in time to help hold Petersburg against the attack made by Union general Burnside, fought at Cold Harbor, and continued to hold part of the lines around Petersburg until early 1865 when he and his remaining troops were sent back to North Carolina in an attempt to defend the state during the final days of the war.

After the war, Hoke engaged in business and helped develop industry in his home state. He was known, lifelong, as a modest man.

The farewell address Hoke issued to his troops is an eloquent piece of writing and it introduces two themes not found in other such documents. First, Hoke was well aware that the Army of Northern Virginia had already established itself in history and in legend as the premier fighting force of the War Between the States. Although he and his men had served for several months in North Carolina on independent duty and, at the end, as part of Joseph Johnston's army, their pride was founded in their service with Lee and the Virginia army:

> ... amid the imperishable laurels
> that surround your brows, no
> brighter leaf adorns them than
> your connection with the late
> Army of Northern Virginia.

The passage of time has confirmed Hoke's estimate of the place of the Army of Northern Virginia in history.

Second, Hoke stated that their fight had been made in the cause of "constitutional freedom." The theme of upholding the Constitution was often sounded by Southerners before the war. Hoke repeats it at the close.

The original foundation document for the United States, the basis on which the colonies declared their independence and then governed themselves for more than a decade, was the Articles of Confederation. Under this document almost all power was reserved to the states and the central government had only very limited powers.

Our first national government was a States' Rights confederacy.

When the Constitution replaced the Articles in 1787 the stated purpose of the new arrangement was to "achieve a more perfect union."

Certain important questions were left unanswered in the Constitution, among them, the
balance of power between the states and the
national government.

Not only was this question unanswered, the
Constitution contained a contradiction. Article
1, Section 6 says that Congress is empowered
"to make all laws which shall be necessary and
proper for carrying into Execution the foregoing
Powers, and all other Powers vested by this
Constitution in the government of the United
States, or in any Department or Officer thereof."
This language aroused opposition from those
who feared the creation of a central government
that would be so large and so strong as to destroy or severely limit the powers of the states.
In the *Federalist Papers, No. 44,* James Madison
and Alexander Hamilton agreed that the "necessary and proper" clause extended only to the
powers enumerated in the Constitution. To
solidify this limiting of power the Bill of Rights
states, in the 10th Amendment, that "The powers not delegated to the United States by the
Constitution, nor prohibited by it to the States,
are reserved to the States respectively, or to the
people."

During the nineteenth century the question
had arisen again and again about what was, or
was not, authorized by the "necessary and

proper clause" and what authority was in the power of the states. Arguments had arisen over the ownership of western lands, whether or not the national government could undertake internal improvements (such as roads) which crossed state lines, the placing of tariffs on imported goods, and the regulation of slavery. Generally, support for the Tenth Amendment was strong in the South where the phrase "States' Rights" summed up the policy of limiting the power of the Federal Government while support for increasing federal power was stronger in the North. The *Dred Scott* decision by the Supreme Court of the United States ruled that slavery was an issue to be decided by the states.

Hoke, in stating that he and his men had fought for constitutional freedom, was referencing state verses federal power. Since the end of the war, the course of government has clearly been toward increasing federal power so that the words of Hoke's address sound prophetic. The defeat of the Confederacy meant the supremacy of the Federal Government over the states and a decline in the political power of the states.

Epilogue

Why Did They Fight?

Lessons from *The Last Words*

None of the 10 Northern states (there were at least 10) whose legislatures responded to the secession crisis by adopting resolutions on the issue expressed a desire to have a war to end slavery. Those states were: New York, New Jersey, Pennsylvania, Ohio, Minnesota, Wisconsin, Michigan, Massachusetts, Indiana and Maine. On the contrary, they accepted the presence of slavery and offered to adopt additional safeguards to protect its existence. For these states the important issue was to preserve the Union.[136]

Gary Gallagher, in his book *The Union War,* argues that preserving the Union was the primary motive for going to war in the North. Gal-

---

[136] Phil Leigh, https://civilwarchat.wordpress.com: The Northern States are clear that they have no desire to go to war to end slavery. This, and other factors, are discussed in detail on the following dates on Phil Leigh's blog: July 12, 13, 14, 15, 16, 18, 2018, accessed August 27, 2018.

lagher does believe that the motivation changed following the Emancipation Proclamation of 1863. The farewell addresses of Union officers say Professor Gallagher is wrong. Preserving the Union remained their primary focus.

The research of James McPherson in his books, *For Cause & Comrades: Why Men Fought In The Civil War,* and *What They Fought For: 1861-1865,* has already been cited. [42] McPherson found that only 5% of Union letters expressed opposition to slavery, and only 10% of Confederate letters even mentioned slavery.

In 1861, had Lincoln called for 75,000 volunteers to fight a war to end slavery, the enlistment quota would not have been filled. People in the North were not interested in going to war to end slavery. At the end of the war, they were still declaring that slavery was not the reason they fought, so the end of slavery must be seen as a byproduct of the war, not its objective.

As stated in the Introduction to this book:

> [A]nyone touring a battlefield
> cannot find a single monument to
> Union soldiers which boasts that
> the men fought to end slavery.
> Their monuments all honor the
> bravery of those who fought, and

they speak of preserving the
Union. Perhaps this emphasis on
preserving the Union is why
historians almost always call the
United States forces the "Union"
army; or the Federals, for
attempting to establish the
supremacy of the Federal
Government over the states,
despite the fact that these names
displace slavery as the central
factor supposedly causing the war.

Only one Union farewell address in this
book mentions slavery as the primary issue of
the war, the address put out by the War Department on behalf of Ulysses S. Grant, which Grant
never signed.

Slavery had been a contentious issue which
had agitated politics for forty years prior to the
war but it was an issue entangled with many
others. There would have been no significant
growth in the numbers of people enslaved had
there not been an insatiable demand in the
North for cotton to support the exploding New
England textile industry and an even greater
demand created by the British textile industry.
Economics and economic advantage played a

huge, arguably decisive, role in creating the conflict.

The larger issue was federal verses state power but race was also an issue, though the attitudes of white Northerners and Southerners were virtually the same about race. That's why the vast majority of white Americans did not view slavery as a moral issue.

The condemnation of the Confederacy and the South as damned by the sin of slavery is selective moral outrage. Northern wealth and power were largely the result of manufacturing for the South (the North's captive market) and shipping Southern slave-picked cotton.

Besides, Northerners had always been America's slave traders, especially New Englanders, people like Peter Faneuil, namesake of Boston's Faneuil Hall. Northerners, and the British before them, brought most of the slaves here through the horrible "Middle Passage," and they had gotten their slave cargoes from blacks in Africa who had sold other blacks into slavery, the result of tribal warfare.

Some will argue that slavery was immoral, therefore the Confederacy was immoral. Such an argument rests on the fallacy historians call "presentism," the application of the standards of today to the people of the past. Certainly, slavery is immoral by the standards of the twenty-first century but was it by the standards of the nineteenth? Clearly not, since many nations accepted the practice of slavery for much of that century.

It should be remembered that what we often call *morality* is actually *mores,* the accepted practices of a society at a given time. *Mores* change. In the lifetime of many living today, the *mores* dealing with the role of women, with abortion, and with same-sex relations have changed dramatically. The attitude of many people today on these issues is quite different from those of the nineteenth century. Shall we condemn the people of the nineteenth century (and all earlier centuries) as sexist, anti-feminist, and homophobic? Or should we admit that our ideas about what is acceptable and unacceptable change?

The answer is obvious and should be applied to the practice of slavery as well.

The misguided efforts to remove Confederate monuments to war dead because of presentism, are disgraceful and political. They are the result of a mob mentality and not based on historical truth.

Confederate monuments are often condemned because many were erected during the period of Jim Crow. Those monuments were put up during a time when laws requiring the separation of the races were becoming common as the nineteenth century reached its last two decades.

Some states had adopted segregation laws before the war, the first of them being Massachusetts. In 1850 the supreme court of that state ruled in the case *Roberts v. City of Boston*, that separate public schools for African American children did not violate the state constitution. In 1896 the Supreme Court of the United States, in *Plessy v. Ferguson*, ruled that separate but equal facilities did not violate the U.S. Constitution and cited *Roberts v. City of Boston* as a precedent. Jim Crow is a native of Massachusetts!

Jim Crow, enforced by law, lasted until 1954 when the Supreme Court issued its ruling in *Brown, et al. v. Board of Education of Topeka, Kansas*. By this time thirty-five states had racial segregation laws, meaning segregation supported by law was not confined to the states of the old Confederacy. Segregation, as a practice or social custom, was practiced universally across the nation.

The period when Jim Crow laws existed did see a huge increase in the number of monuments being erected but is there any direct connection?

By 1896, the year the Supreme Court issued

Plessy v. Ferguson, the war had been over 31 years. The veterans, North and South, were aging and they expressed a strong desire to see that their deeds were not forgotten. So great was the demand for monuments that the number of companies producing statues of soldiers of the War Between the States increased from four to sixty-three. The products of these companies were sold nationwide. Between 1890 and 1920, sixteen such monuments were erected in Washington, D.C. alone—all of them to Union soldiers. Between 1900 and 1910, massive monuments were put up in Columbus, Ohio; Des Moins, Iowa; Indianapolis, Indiana; Springfield, Illinois, and other places. Some of these places had Jim Crow laws, and all of them practiced racial segregation by custom and tradition.

Jim Crow was not born in Dixie and neither did he speak only with a Southern drawl. The contention that since Confederate monuments were erected during the era of Jim Crow they must have some connection to *de jure* segregation rests on a logical fallacy, *post hoc, ergo, propter hoc,* "after this, therefore, because of this." An honest reading of the history of the period completely disproves the assertion.

The people who erected war memorials, North and South, were mourning war dead and paying tribute to American valor. Only rarely did any speaker at the ceremonies dedicating such monuments say anything which presents the monument as promoting white supremacy, and these examples are found in both the dedications of Union and Confederate monuments.

Overwhelmingly, the speakers at dedication ceremonies said the monuments were intended to honor those who fought and to remember those who died.

If we are to remove monuments erected by people of the past who believed in white supremacy, we would have to start with the Lincoln Memorial in Washington, D.C., then *all* the monuments of the War Between the States, North and South, as well as monuments to the Indian fighters who conquered the West. Monuments to George Washington and Thomas Jefferson would have to go too. Of course, this is absurd, ridiculous and disgusting.

Removing century-old monuments to war dead is a criminal act committed by politically motivated people today, a theft of art and history belonging to people of the future who are being robbed of the opportunity to contemplate the past and American's bloodiest war.

The words of Nathan Bedford Forrest in the farewell address to his command offered sound advice, which was followed by North and South after the war, and should continue to be followed by *all* Americans today, regardless of politics or skin color:

> Civil war, such as you have just passed through, naturally engenders feelings of animosity, hatred, and revenge. It is our duty to divest ourselves of all such feelings and, so far as it is in our power to do so, to cultivate a friendly feeling toward those with whom we have so long contended and heretofore so widely but honestly differed.

Appendix A

The Six Union Slave States

The Emancipation Proclamation deliberately did not free any of the slaves in the six slave states that fought for the Union the entire war. Three of those Union slave states had slavery even beyond the war. Slavery did not end in those three Union slave states until the 13th Amendment, in December, 1865, forced them to end slavery.

The Emancipation Proclamation also did not free any slaves in Confederate territory already captured by the Union at the time it became effective, on January 1, 1863.

Foreigners such as Charles Dickens, laughed at Lincoln for issuing such a document. Even Lincoln's secretary of state, William H. Seward, said "We show our sympathy with slavery by emancipating slaves where we cannot reach them and holding them in bondage where we can set them free."[137]

---

[137] James G. Randall and Donald H. Donald, *The Civil War and Reconstruction* (Lexington, Mass.: D. C. Heath, 1969), 371.

Appendix A
The Six Union Slave States

The Union slave states exempted by the Emancipation Proclamation were Missouri, Kentucky, Maryland, Delaware, New Jersey, and the parts of Virginia that became the Union slave state of West Virginia during the war.

Missouri and Kentucky were divided states and both were claimed by, and had representation in, the Union and Confederate governments. Neither officially left the Union so both were Union slave states throughout the war.

As stated, West Virginia came into the Union as a slave state, ironically, within a few weeks of the issuance of the Emancipation Proclamation. It had a weak plan for gradual emancipation called the Willey Amendment that freed no slaves initially, and would have left thousands of slaves in slavery their entire lives. It would also have left many others as slaves for 20 years before being freed.

Of the six Union slave states, Maryland, Missouri and West Virginia ended slavery close to the end of the war.

The other three states kept their slaves eight-and-a-half months *beyond* the war. The slaves in New Jersey, Kentucky and Delaware were not freed until the 13th Amendment took effect in December, 1865. New Jersey did have a program of gradual emancipation in place but there were still a handful of slaves in New Jersey until the 13th Amendment finally freed them.

The 1860 census showed 225,483 slaves in Kentucky, and 1,798 in Delaware, which is a total of 227,281. Some number of slaves close to that 227,281 remained in bondage eight months beyond the end of the War Between the States in those two Union slave states.

Appendix B

More Detail on Alabama and Arkansas

Alabama's ordinance of secession includes the following passage:

> Whereas, the election of Abraham Lincoln and Hannibal Hamlin to the offices of president and vice-president of the United States of America, by a sectional party, avowedly hostile to the domestic institutions and to the peace and security of the people of the State of Alabama, preceded by many and dangerous infractions of the constitution of the United States by many of the States and people of the Northern section, is a political wrong of so insulting and menacing a character as to justify the people of the State of Alabama in the adoption of prompt and decided measures for their future peace and security . . . .

More Detail on Alabama and Arkansas

Arkansas, at first, rejected secession. They did not secede until after Lincoln called for 75,000 volunteers to invade the South, and the reason they seceded was utter revulsion at the idea that the federal government, now controlled by a Northern sectional party, had the power to invade a sovereign state and kill its citizens to compel it to obey that Northern sectional party.

Arkansas's ordinance of secession does not specifically mention slavery but it does, in the passage below, refer to resolutions passed a few weeks earlier that discussed the slavery issue:

> Whereas, in addition to the well-founded causes of complaint set forth by this convention, in resolutions adopted on the 11th of March, A.D. 1861, [they were actually adopted on the 20th of March 1861, not the 11th] against the sectional party now in power in Washington City, headed by Abraham Lincoln, he has, in the face of resolutions passed by this convention pledging the State of Arkansas to resist to the last extremity any attempt on the part of such power to coerce any State that had seceded from the old

Union, proclaimed to the world
that war should be waged against
such States until they should be
compelled to submit to their rule,
and large forces to accomplish this
have by this same power been
called out, and are now being
marshaled to carry out this
inhuman design; and to longer
submit to such rule, or remain in
the old Union of the United States,
would be disgraceful and ruinous
to the State of Arkansas . . . .

Bibliography

Acton, John Dalberg, to Gen. Robert E. Lee. November 4, 1866. The Acton-Lee Correspondence. https://www.lewrockwell.com/ 2017/09/no_author/famed-libertarian-writes-robert-e-lee. Accessed May 3, 2020.

Acton, John Emerich Edward Dalberg. 1st Baron Acton (born 1834, died 1902). https://www.britannica.com/biography/John -Emerich-Edward-Dalberg-Acton-1st-Baron-Acton. Accessed May 3, 2020.

Address of the People of South Carolina, Assembled in Convention, to the People of the Slaveholding States of the United States. Written by Robert Barnwell Rhett, adopted 24 December 1860 by the South Carolina Secession Convention, Charleston, S.C. In May, John Amasa, and Joan Reynolds Faunt, *South Carolina Secedes*. Columbia, SC: University of South Carolina Press, 1960, 82-92.

Archives, National. Washington, DC. Union Provost Marshal Records. File of Individual Citizens, Microfilm Collection, Microfilm Roll 285.

Barefoot, Daniel W. *General Robert F. Hoke: Lee's Modest General.* Winston-Salem: John F. Blair, Publisher, 1996.

Basler, Roy P., ed. *The Collected Works of Abraham Lincoln.* New Brunswick, NJ: Rutgers University Press, 1953.

Bates, Delvan. Letter to his father. June 27, 1864. *Bates Letters.* U.S. Army Center for Military History.

Bledsoe, Albert Taylor. *Is Davis A Traitor; or Was Secession a Constitutional Right Previous to The War of 1861?* Baltimore: Innes & Company, 1866; reprint, North Charleston, SC: Fletcher and Fletcher Publishing, 1995.

Bloom, Allan. *The Closing of the American Mind: How Higher Education Has Failed Democracy and Impoverished the Souls of Today's Students.* New York: Simon and Schuster, 1987.

Boles, John B. and Evelyn Thomas Nolen. *Interpreting Southern History: Historiographical Essays in Honor of Sanford W. Higginbotham.* Baton Rouge: Louisiana State University Press, 1987.

Bradley, Mark L. *This Astounding Close: The Road to Bennett Place.* Chapel Hill: University of North Carolina Press, 2000.

Bradley, Michael R. *With Blood and Fire: Behind Union Lines in Middle Tennessee, 1863-1865.* Shippensburg, PA: Burd Street Press, 2003.

Brown, John (slave trader). In *United States Chronicle,* March 26, 1789. Providence, Rhode Island. In Farrow, Anne, et al. *Complicity, How the North Promoted, Prolonged, and Profited from Slavery.* New York: Ballantine Books, 2005 (by The Hartford Courant Company), 110.

Christian Recorder. July 9, 1864. The *Christian Recorder,* founded in 1852, is "The official organ of the African Methodist Episcopal Church."

Cogswell, William. "An Eloquent Farewell Address to His Troops by a Massachusetts General." www.SethKaller.com. Accessed July 10, 2020.

Cohen, Jennie. "Civil War Deadlier Than Previously Thought?" https://www.history.com/news/civil-war-deadlier-than-previously-thought. Accessed 3-8-22.

Coker, Rachel. "Historian revises estimate of Civil War dead." September 21, 2011. Binghamton University Research News. http://discovere.binghamton.edu/news/civilwar-3826.html. Accessed July 7, 2014.

Continental Monthly. "The Slave-Trade in New York." January, 1862. https://www.gutenberg.org/files/18977/18977-h/18977-h.htm#THE_SLAVE-TRADE_IN_NEW_YORK. Accessed 7-6-22

Cureton, T. J. Letter to Colonel J. R. Lane 22 June 1890. *Lane Papers.* In Archie K. Davis, *Boy Colonel of the Confederacy, The Life and Times of Henry King Burgwyn, Jr.* Chapel Hill: The University of North Carolina Press, 1985, Appendix, 351.

Daily Chicago Times. "The Value of the Union." December 10, 1860. In Perkins, Howard Cecil, ed., *Northern Editorials on Secession*, Vol. II, Gloucester, MA: Peter Smith, 1964, 571-575.

Davis, Archie K. *Boy Colonel of the Confederacy: The Life and Times of Henry King Burgwyn, Jr.* Chapel Hill: The University of North Carolina Press, 1985.

Davis, Burke. *Sherman's March.* New York: Random House, 1980.

Declaration of the Immediate Causes Which Induce and Justify the Secession of South Carolina from the Federal Union, The. Adopted December 24, 1860 by S.C.'s secession convention. Written by Christopher Memminger.

Dickens, Charles. Letter to W. W. De Cerjat. 16 March 1862. In Storey, Graham, ed. *The Letters of Charles Dickens.* Oxford, UK: Clarendon Press, 1998, Vol. 10, 1862-1864, 53-54.

Dobak, William A. *Freedom by the Sword.* Washington, DC: Center of Military History, U.S. Army, 2011.

Downs, Jim. *Sick from Freedom: African-American Illness and Suffering During the Civil War and Reconstruction*. Oxford, UK: Oxford University Press, 2012.

Du Bois, W. E. B. *The Suppression of the African Slave-Trade to the United States of America: 1638-1870*. New York: Longmans, Green and Co., 1896.

Eisenhower, Dwight D. Letter, August 9, 1960, to Leon W. Scott. "Dwight D. Eisenhower in Defense of Robert E. Lee." August 10, 2014. Mathew W. Lively, https://www.civilwarprofiles.com/dwight-d-eisenhower-in-defense-of-robert-e-lee. Accessed 5-3-20.

Farrow, Anne, et al. *Complicity, How the North Promoted, Prolonged, and Profited from Slavery*. New York: Ballantine Books, 2005 (by The Hartford Courant Company).

Faust, Drew Gilpin. *This Republic of Suffering: Death and the American Civil War*. New York: Alfred A. Knopf, 2008.

FindLaw. Executor of a will.
https://estate.findlaw.com/estate-
administration/what-does-an-executor-
do.html. Accessed May 10, 2020.

Foner, Eric. *Reconstruction: America's Unfinished Revolution, 1863-1877.* New York:
Harper Perennial, 2014. Originally published,
1988.

Forrest, Nathan Bedford. *Nathan Bedford Forrest Farewell Address.* John A. Wyeth. *That
Devil Forrest.* New York: Harper & Bros.,
1899, 613-14.

Fox, William F. *Regimental Losses in the American Civil War.* Albany, NY: Joseph McDonough, 1898.

Freehling, William W. and Craig M. Simpson.
*Secession Debated, Georgia's Showdown in
1860.* New York: Oxford University Press,
1992.

Freeman, Douglas Southall. *R. E. Lee: A Biography.* 4 vols. New York: Charles Scribner's
Sons, 1936.

Gallagher, Gary. *The Union War*. Cambridge: Harvard University Press, 2011.

Galveston Tri-Weekly News, June 5, 1865. In Joseph H. Parks *General Edmund Kirby Smith, C.S.A.* Baton Rouge: LSU Press, 1954, 475-76.

Gates, Henry Louis, Jr. "Ending the Slavery Blame-Game." *New York Times*, April 22, 2010. https://www.nytimes.com/2010/04/23/opinion/23gates.html. Accessed 5-21-22.

Genovese, Eugene D. *The Southern Tradition: The Achievement and Limitations of an American Conservatism*. Cambridge: Harvard University Press, 1994.

Georgia Convention, Journal of. Journal of the Public and Secret Proceedings of the Convention of the People of Georgia, Held in Milledgeville and Savannah in 1861, Together with the Ordinances Adopted.

Gerteis, Louis S. *From Contraband to Freedman: Federal Policy Toward Southern Blacks 1861-1865*. Westport, CT: Greenwood Press, 1973.

Gibson, Randall L. "Farewell Address to the Louisiana Brigade." *Southern Historical Society Papers*. Richmond: Southern Historical Society, 1917, Vol. 4, 223-4.

Gildersleeve, Basil L. *The Creed of the Old South*. Baltimore: The Johns Hopkins Press, 1915; reprint: BiblioLife, Penrose Library, University of Denver (no date given).

Grand Army of Black Men: Letters from African-American Soldiers in the Union Army 1861–1865. Edwin S. Redkey, ed. Cambridge Studies in American Literature and Culture, 1992.

Grant, Julia Dent. *The Personal Memoirs of Julia Dent Grant (Mrs. Ulysses S. Grant)*. John Y. Simon, ed. Carbondale, Illinois: Southern Illinois University Press 1975 by the Ulysses S. Grant Association.

Grant, Ulysses S. "10 Things You May Not Know About Ulysses S. Grant." Updated April 7, 2020. https://www.history.com/news/10-things-you-may-not-know-about-ulysses-s-grant. Accessed April 21, 2020.

Grant, Ulysses S. March 30, 2020 (updated). https://www.history.com/topics/us-presidents/ulysses-s-grant-1. Accessed April 21, 2020.

Guelzo, Allen C. "George Meade's Mixed Legacy." *The Cupola.* June 2013. Published by Gettysburg College, 40-41.

Harlan, David. *The Degradation of American History.* Chicago: University of Chicago Press, 1997.

Hooper, Candice Shy. "The Two Julias." February 14, 2013. *The New York Times.* Original location: https://opinionator.blogs.nytimes.com/2013/02/14/the-twojulias. Accessed April 10, 2020.

Howard, O. O. *Autobiography of Oliver Otis Howard,* Vol. 2. New York: Baker and Taylor, 1907, 364.

Jones, J. William. *Southern Historical Society Papers.* 52 vols. Richmond: Southern Historical Society. Reprint: Broadfoot Publishing Company, 1990.

Jordan, Thomas, and J. P. Pryor. *The Campaigns of General Nathan Bedford Forrest and of Forrest's Cavalry.* New York: Da Capo Press, 1996. Originally published 1886.

Kennedy, John F. Speech of Senator John F. Kennedy. Raleigh, NC, September 17, 1960. Coliseum Online by Gerhard Peters and John T. Woolley. The American Presidency Project. https://www.presidency.ucsb.edu/documents/speech-senator-john-f-kennedy-raleigh-nc-coliseum. Accessed 5/3/2020.

Keystone Brigade. "Farewell Address to the Keystone Brigade." Field Printed Broadside. www.HCAAuctions.com. Accessed June 20, 2018.

Leigh, Philip. "Did Ulysses Grant Own and Rent Slaves?" February 8, 2019. https://www.abbevilleinstitute.org/blog/did-ulysses-grant-own-and-rent-slaves. Accessed April 9, 2020.

_____. "Ketanji Jackson and the Confederate Flag." Civil War Chat. https://civilwarchat.wordpress.com/2022/03/21/ketanji-jackson-and-the-confederate-flag. Accessed 3-22-22.

_____. "New York Replies to Southern Se-
cession."
https://civilwarchat.wordpress.com/2018/07
/16/new-york-replies-to-southern-secession.
July 16, 2018. Accessed July 18, 2018.

_____. Northern states no desire for war to
end slavery. This, and other factors discussed
in detail on the following dates on Phil
Leigh's blog: July 12, 13, 14, 15, 16, 18, 2018.
https://civilwarchat.wordpress.com.
Accessed August 27, 2018.

_____. "President Grant's Doubtful Civil
Rights Motives." February 3, 2018.
https://civilwarchat.wordpress.com/2018/02
/03/president-grants-doubtful-civil-rights-
motives. Accessed April 10, 2020.

_____. "Why Pennsylvania Chose Civil War."
https://civilwarchat.wordpress.com/2018/07
/13/why-pennsylvania-chose-civil-war, July
13, 2018. Accessed July 4, 2020.

Leigh, Philip. *U.S. Grant's Failed Presidency.*
Columbia, SC: Shotwell Publishing, 2019.

Lincoln, Abraham. Letter. A. Lincoln to Horace
Greeley, August 22, 1862. In Basler, Roy P.,
ed. *The Collected Works of Abraham Lincoln*.
New Brunswick, NJ: Rutgers University
Press, 1953, V:388.

Livingston, Donald W. "The Secession Tradition
in America." David Gordon, ed., *Secession,
State & Liberty*. New Brunswick NJ: Transaction Publishers, 2002.

Mann, Maria R. To Elisa, February 10, 1863; to
Miss Peabody, April 19, 1863. *Maria Mann
Papers*, Library of Congress. In Gerteis, Louis
S. *From Contraband to Freedman: Federal
Policy Toward Southern Blacks 1861-1865*.
Westport, CT: Greenwood Press, 1973, 121, in
Downs, Jim. *Sick from Freedom: African-
American Illness and Suffering During the
Civil War and Reconstruction*. Oxford, UK:
Oxford University Press, 2012, 27.

May, John Amasa, and Joan Reynolds Faunt,
South Carolina Secedes. Columbia, SC: University of South Carolina Press, 1960.

McPherson, James M. *Battle Cry of Freedom:
The Civil War Era*. New York: Oxford University Press, 1988.

_____. *Crossroads of Freedom: Antietam.* New York: Oxford University Press, 2002.

_____. *For Cause & Comrades: Why Men Fought In The Civil War.* New York: Oxford University Press, 1997.

_____. *What They Fought For: 1861-1865.* New York: Random House, 1994.

Meade, George G. *Life & Letters of George Gordon Meade, Major General–U.S. Army.* New York: Charles Scribner's Sons.

Missouri, Constitution of 1865 - Drake Constitution. http://www.civilwarmo.org/ educators/resources/info-sheets/ constitution-1865-drake-constitution. Accessed May 5, 2020.

Missouri State Archives. Guide to African American History. https://www.sos.mo.gov/ archives/resources/africanamerican/guide/ image005c. Accessed May 4, 2020.

Missouri State Archives. Missouri Constitutions, 1820-1945. http://mdh.contentdm.oclc.org/ cdm/landingpage/collection/p16795coll1. Accessed May 5, 2020.

Missouri, An Ordinance Abolishing Slavery in, https://www.sos.mo.gov/CMSImages/MDH /1865ConstitutionOrdinanceabolishingslaver yinMissouri.pdf. Accessed May 4, 2020.

Mitcham, Samuel W., Jr. *It Wasn't About Slavery: Exposing the Great Lie of the Civil War.* Washington, DC: Regnery History, 2020.

Mitchell, A. L. to John Eaton. May 31, 1864. *Extracts from Reports of Superintendents of the Freedmen,* compiled by Rev. Joseph Warren in Downs, Jim. *Sick from Freedom: African-American Illness and Suffering During the Civil War and Reconstruction.* Oxford, UK: Oxford University Press, 2012, 21, 24.

Mosby's Farewell Address. April 21, 1865. *J. Henley Smith Papers.* Library of Congress.

Mosby, John S. "John S. Mosby on Slavery as the Cause of the War." Original location: www.ThisCruelWar.com. September 13, 2016. Accessed July 11, 2018.

New-York Daily Tribune, The. "The Right of Secession." December 17, 1860. In Perkins, Howard Cecil, ed., *Northern Editorials on Secession,* Vol. I, Gloucester, MA: Peter Smith, 1964, 199-201.

New York Herald. Editorial. April 5, 1861. In Mitcham, Samuel W., Jr. *It Wasn't About Slavery: Exposing the Great Lie of the Civil War*. Washington, DC: Regnery History, 2020, 147.

New York Tribune. June 24, 1864. "The Assault on Petersburg — Valor of the Colored Troops — They Take No Prisoners and Leave No Wounded."

Orwell, George. *1984*. New York: New American Library, 1950.

Parks, Joseph H. *General Edmund Kirby Smith, C.S.A.* Baton Rouge: LSU Press, 1954.

Perkins, Howard Cecil, ed., *Northern Editorials on Secession*. Gloucester, MA: Peter Smith, 1964.

Preliminary Emancipation Proclamation. September 22,1862. https://www.archives.gov/exhibits/american_originals_iv/sections/transcript_preliminary_emancipation.html. Accessed 4-12-22.

Ramsdell, Charles W. *Charles W. Ramsdell, Dean of Southern Historians, Volume One: His Best Work*. Charleston, SC: Charleston Athenaeum Press, 2017.

Randall, James G. and David H. Donald. *The Civil War and Reconstruction*. Lexington, MA: D. C. Heath, 1969.

Report on the Causes of the Secession of Georgia. Adopted by the Georgia Secession Convention. Tuesday, 29 January 1861.

Robbins, James S. *Erasing America: Losing Our Future by Destroying Our Past*. Washington, DC: Regnery Publishing, 2018.

Robison, Brevet Colonel J. K. - Gasbarro, Norman. *16th Pennsylvania Cavalry - Farewell Address*. "An address by Brevet Colonel J. K. Robison, of the 16th Pennsylvania Cavalry." http://civilwar.gratzpa.org/2011/07/16th-pennsylvania-cavalry-farewell-address. July 27, 2011. Accessed July 6, 2020.

Saxton, Rufus B. "General Saxton Protests Against the Forced Enlistment of Freed Slaves." *After Slavery: Educator Resources*. Accessed June 18, 2018.

Seven Pines, Battle of. Also known as the Battle of Fair Oaks, or Battle of Fair Oaks Station. May 31 to June 1, 1862. https://www.encyclopediavirginia.org/seven_pines_battle_of. Accessed May 17, 2020.

Sherman, William T., to Stanton. June 21, 1864. *O.R.*, Series 1, Vol. 39, Part 2.

Sherman, William T., to his wife. May 8, 1865. *Sherman Family Papers.* In Bradley, Mark L. *This Astounding Close: The Road to Bennett Place.* Chapel Hill: University of North Carolina Press, 2000, 171-172.

Sherwood, Isaac. *Farewell Address of Isaac Sherwood to the 111th Ohio Infantry.* June 27, 1865. Ohio History Center, Box 55, Catalog #4556.

Simon, John Y., ed. *Papers of Ulysses Grant.* 31 vols. Carbondale: Southern Illinois University Press, 1967.

Slocum, Charles Elihu. *The Life and Services of Major General Henry Warner Slocum.* Toledo: Slocum Publishing Co., 1913.

Slocum, General. Timeline.
http://www.union12thcorps.com/slocum-timeline.html. Accessed August 15, 2018.

Slocum, Maj. Gen. Henry W., Speech. June, 1865. Syracuse, New York.
http://www.armyofgeorgia.com/id22.html. Accessed August 10, 2018.

Stokes, Chip. "Company B, North Carolina 71st Infantry Regiment....",
http://blueandgrayancestors.blogspot.com/2013/05/company-b-north-carolina-2nd-junior.html. May 20, 2013. Accessed 7-10-20.

Storey, Graham, ed. *The Letters of Charles Dickens*. Oxford, UK: Clarendon Press, 1998.

Taylor, Joe Gray. "The White South from Secession to Redemption." In Boles, John B. and Evelyn Thomas Nolen *Interpreting Southern History: Historiographical Essays in Honor of Sanford W. Higginbotham.* Baton Rouge: Louisiana State University Press, 1987, 162-164.

Times. Florence, Alabama. "Wheeler's Farewell Address." September 21, 1900.

Tocqueville, Alexis de. *Democracy in America.* 1835, 1840. New York: Alfred A. Knopf (1945), Everyman's Library, 1994.

Toombs, Robert. "Secessionist Speech, Tuesday Evening, November 13" delivered to the Georgia legislature in Milledgeville. November 13, 1860.

Trowbridge, Charles Taylor. "Six Months in the Freedmans Bureau with a Colored Regiment." *Papers of the Minnesota Commandery of the Military Order of the Loyal Legion of the United States*, Series 6, Vol. 32, No. 1.

United States Census Bureau, The. "Eighth Census under the Secretary of the Interior." https://www.census.gov/history/www/through_the_decades/fast_facts/1860_fast_facts.html. Accessed 3-7-22.

Vernon, Charles T. Letter to his father. *Grand Army of Black Men: Letters from African-American Soldiers in the Union Army 1861–1865*. Edwin S. Redkey, ed. Cambridge Studies in American Literature and Culture, 1992, 99.

War Aims Resolution. Also known by the names
    of its sponsors, Representative John. J. Crit-
    tenden of Kentucky and Senator Andrew
    Johnson of Tennessee: The Crittenden-John-
    son Resolution, or just the Crittenden Reso-
    lution. http://en.wikipedia.org/wiki/
    Crittenden-Johnson_Resolution.
    Accessed April 19, 2022.

War of the Rebellion, The: A Compilation of the
    Official Records of the Union and Confederate
    Armies (O.R.). Washington: Government
    Printing Office, 1880, 1900; reprint, Historical
    Times Inc., 1985.

Wilson, Clyde. Review of John Lukacs *Historical*
    Consciousness, or the Remembered Past.
    Schocken Books, 1985. The Abbeville Review.
    February 12, 2019.
    https://www.abbevilleinstitute.org/review/hi
    storical-consciousness. Accessed
    February 12, 2019.

Windschuttle, Keith. *The Killing of History: How*
    Literary Critics and Social Theorists Are Mur-
    dering Our Past. New York: The Free Press,
    1996.

Wise, Henry A. "The Career of Wise's Brigade."
Southern Historical Society Papers, Vol. 25, 13.

Wood, Peter W. *1620: A Critical Response to the
1619 Project*. New York: Encounter Books,
2020.

Wyeth, John A. *That Devil Forrest*. New York:
Harper & Bros., 1899.

Zeller, Bob. "How Many Died in the American
Civil War?" January 6, 2022.
https://www.history.com/news/american-
civil-war-deaths. Accessed 3-8-22.

About the Author

Michael R. Bradley is a native of the Tennessee-Alabama state line region near Fayetteville, TN. He earned a B.A. from Samford University, a Master of Divinity at New Orleans Seminary, and an M.A. and Ph.D. from Vanderbilt University.

For thirty-six years, Dr. Bradley taught United States History at Motlow College near Tullahoma, Tennessee. He has been pastor of two Presbyterian churches in Middle Tennessee and interim Pastor of two others.

Dr. Bradley is the author of several books on the War Between the States in Tennessee and Nathan Bedford Forrest, but he has written on topics ranging from the Revolutionary War to death in the Great Smoky Mountains.

His books include: *They Rode with Forrest; Tullahoma: The 1863 Campaign for the Control of Middle Tennessee; With Blood and Fire: Life Behind Union Lines in Middle Tennessee, 1863-65; Nathan Bedford Forrest's Escort & Staff in War and Peace; It Happened in the Revolutionary War; It Happened in the Civil War: Remarkable Events That Shaped History; Myths and Mysteries of the Civil War; Forrest's Fighting Preacher, David Campbell Kelley of Tennessee; The Raiding Winter; Civil War Myths and Legends: The True Stories Behind History's Mysteries; Death in the Great Smoky Mountains*, and others along with a lifetime of articles and talks.

In 1994 he was awarded the Jefferson Davis Medal in Southern History. In 2006 he was elected commander of the Tennessee Division SCV and is a Life Member. He was appointed by Gov. Phil Bredesen to Tennessee's Civil War Sesquicentennial Commission.

Dr. Bradley is married with two adult children, two grandsons and one granddaughter. He lives with his wife, Martha, in Tullahoma.

Colophon

Editing and page layout were done by
Gene Kizer, Jr. with Atlantis Word Processor.

The main body text is CenturionOld, 12 point,
with 1.1 leading. The title page and half titles are
Leamington-Light and the drop caps are Old
English.

The front cover was designed by the publisher
working with artists through 99Designs.com.

The battle in the picture on the front cover is the
Battle of Franklin, Tennessee, November 30,
1864 (Kurz & Allison, 1891).

Published in 2022 by

Charleston Athenaeum Press

Other Books from
Charleston Athenaeum Press

www.CharlestonAthenaeumPress.com

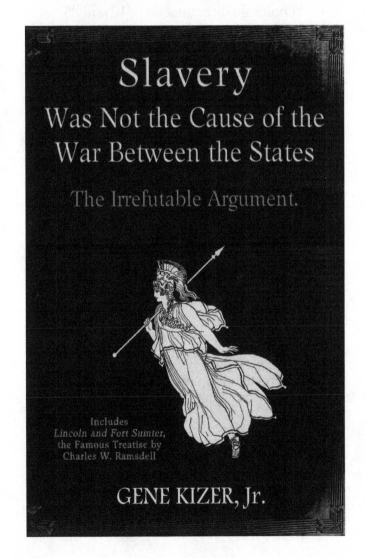

Slavery

Was Not the Cause of the
War Between the States

The Irrefutable Argument.

Includes
Lincoln and Fort Sumter,
the Famous Treatise by
Charles W. Ramsdell

GENE KIZER, Jr.

- 360 pages, 218 footnotes, 207 sources in the bibliography
- 236 reviews on Amazon and a 4.6 out of 5 rating as of May 28, 2022
- Wholesale discounts on 5, 10 and 25 copies, and other Specials
- **Fabulously Crafted Kindle ebook** on Amazon.com that includes all 218 footnotes and the bibliography

ISBN: 978-0-9853632-7-7 *(print)*
ISBN: 978-0-9853632-6-0 *(ebook)*

Testimonial

Historians used to know - and it was not too long ago - that the War Between the States had more to do with economics than it did with slavery. The current obsession with slavery as the "cause" of the war rests not on evidence but on ideological considerations of the present day. Gene Kizer has provided us with the conclusive case that the invasion of the Southern States by Lincoln and his party (a minority of the American people) was due to an agenda of

economic domination and not to
some benevolent concern for
slaves. This book is rich in
evidence and telling quotations
and ought to be on every Southern
bookshelf.

Clyde N. Wilson
Emeritus Distinguished Professor of History
University of South Carolina

- Part I, *The Irrefutable Argument,* makes
  the "conclusive" case that the North did
  not go to war to free the slaves or end
  slavery. They went to war because they
  faced economic annihilation of their own
  doing.
- Part II is *The Right of Secession,* docu-
  menting and proving that States had the
  right to secede from the Union (e.g., New
  York, Rhode Island and Virginia specifically reserved the right of secession
  before acceding to the U.S. Constitution
  thus giving that right to all the States;
  MUCH more solid proof provided).
- Part III is the famous treatise *Lincoln and
  Fort Sumter* by Charles W. Ramsdell
  proving with fascinating scholarly detail
  how Lincoln set things up in Charleston

Harbor to start a war. Lincoln also committed acts of war at the same time in Pensacola, Florida at Fort Pickens by landing troops and breaking an armistice. Several Northern newspapers agreed that Lincoln's goal was to start hostilities including the *Providence (R.I.) Daily Post* and the *New York Herald. Lincoln and Fort Sumter* also includes the diary entry from Lincoln's friend, Orville H. Browning, July 3, 1861, in which Lincoln, not knowing Browning would record it all in his private diary, admitted what he had done to get the war started.

- Includes "An Annotated Chronology of the Secession Debate in the South," a day-by-day account of speeches, convention dates, ratification votes, birth of the Confederate States of America, beginning of the war, and secession of the final Southern States.
- Includes a powerful "Introduction" full of history to kick off the argument, and "Author's Final Assessment" to conclude it.
- Includes a section devoted to further study: "Additional Resources for the Study of Southern History and Literature."

Testimonial

Gene Kizer persuasively shows
how the North fought the South
out of necessity to prevent
economic collapse. No where else
is proof of this motive made
clearer with indisputable evidence.
Mr. Kizer writes with authority
from the desire to tell the truth.
His common sense style is the
product of honesty. One cannot
read his work without concluding
that this is a man to be trusted.

James Everett Kibler
Critically acclaimed novelist, poet,
historian, and literary scholar

Author of
Our Fathers' Fields; Walking Toward Home;
and many other outstanding books.

Charles W. Ramsdell
Dean of Southern Historians

Volume One:
His Best Work

**Includes Legendary
*Lincoln and Fort Sumter;
The Natural Limits of Slavery
Expansion; Carl Sandburg's
Lincoln;* and Six Other
Brilliant Treatises, with 15
Reviews of Books Written by
Famous Historians.**

Compiled, and with Introduction by

GENE KIZER, Jr.

"In all that pertained to the history of the Southern Confederacy, his scholarship was decisive."

*In Memoriam
Charles William Ramsdell*
University of Texas

- Includes the famous treatises "Lincoln
  and Fort Sumter" and "The Natural Limits of Slavery Expansion"
- 462 pages, 6 x 9" softcover
- 11 reviews and a 5 out of 5 rating on
  Amazon.com as of 5-29-22

  ISBN: 978-0-9853632-3-9 (*softcover*)

Ramsdell's Book Reviews Are Works of Art

(**Compiler's Note:** Ramsdell's treatises
and reviews are outstanding, written in
a much better era for history than
today's wokism and political
correctness. There is an unbelievable
amount of history in each of Ramsdell's
fifteen book reviews. He had to include
a lot in order to provide background and
put the subject in perspective. Ramsdell
pulls no punches. He reviewed many
more than fifteen books in his career
but in this fifteen are outstanding, well-
known books by distinguished
historians.)

- *R. E. Lee: A Biography*, 4 vols.,
  by Douglas Southall Freeman

- *The Civil War and Reconstruction*,
  by J. G. Randall
- *The Repressible Conflict, 1830—1861*,
  by Avery Craven
- *The American Civil War: An Interpretation*, by Carl Russell Fish
- *State Rights in the Confederacy*,
  by Frank Lawrence Owsley
- *Life and Labor in the Old South*,
  by Ulrich Bonnell Phillips
- *The Story of the Confederacy*,
  by Robert Selph Henry
- *Constitutional Problems under Lincoln*,
  by James G. Randall
- *Guide to the Study and Reading of American History*,
  by Edward Channing, Albert Bushnell Hart, and Frederick J. Turner
- *Bedford Forrest, The Confederacy's Greatest Cavalryman*,
  by Eric William Sheppard
- *Southern Editorials on Secession*,
  compiled by Dwight Lowell Dumond
- *The Secession Movement, 1860—1861*,
  by Dwight Lowell Dumond
- *Aeronautics in the Union and Confederate Armies, With a Survey of Military Aeronautics Prior to 1861*, Vol. I,
  by F. Stansbury Haydon

Other Books from
Charleston Athenaeum Press

- *Lincoln Takes Command,* by John Shipley Tilley
- *John Brown, Soldier of Fortune: A Critique,* by Hill Publes Wilson

The most powerful academic guide since
Strunk and White's classic, *The Elements
of Style,* for high school, college and adult
students.

- 364 page softcover (6 x 9") with 351 numbered topic sections in 10 chapters that are EASY to go through
- Available as a Kindle ebook on Amazon.com
- **Highly beneficial** to high school and college students as well as adults returning to school
- Readers will absorb the author's highly effective skills, techniques and NOT-GOING-TO-BE-DENIED attitude

ISBN: 978-0-9853632-1-5 *(softcover)*
ISBN: 978-0-9853632-2-2 *(ebook)*

Contents
(with each chapter's epigraph)

I
Start Strong
Be Organized and in Control
Page 3

By recording the dates on which you need to START assignments, you give yourself a perfect blueprint for the entire semester, especially those times when things stack up. In college, there are things going on all the time, but you will be able to coordinate everything. Your weeks will be extremely productive and satisfying by planning them around your calendar.

II
Professors
Page 39

Most professors are decent people who enjoy teaching their material and really want you to succeed in their classes, but some are unquestionably better than others, and some are unquestionably harder graders than others. You'll have to decide the best fit for you.

III
Class
Page 68

Write fast, but write down everything that comes out of a professor's mouth. That's what I did at the College of Charleston. It is invaluable to have notes like that when test time rolls around. You have a lot of options for producing homemade study guides from a good set of notes, and at the very least, you will be able to go through your notebook and highlight the most important things, tag pages, etc.

IV
Grades
Page 90

The actual quotation belongs to Confucius:
"Choose a job you love, and you will never have
to work a day in your life." **This is the foundation of all happiness and success.** If you
do what you love, you will be so stimulated by
what you do, it won't seem like work. It will be
fun! So, pursue with all your heart, your dreams
and goals and the things that stimulate you!
Have success, achieve some great things, make
money, find a partner who makes you happy and
live a great life!

V
Studying Effectively
Page 105

Constantly reading, writing, working problems,
researching, thinking, struggling with another
language's vocabulary, and the other challenges
one faces in college, unquestionably increase
intellectual capacity. It's no different from training for a physical competition. One works the
body hard, running, weightlifting, swimming,

bike riding, and as a result, the body gets stronger, faster, healthier, and the individual is happier, more confident, and more powerful. The intellectual rigors of college life increase a student's brain power, and that increased brain power is there for everything in the student's life, from sports, to achievement of personal goals, to wooing a love interest. Brainpower is the key to happiness, and the more one has, the better.

VI
Preparing for Tests/Exams
Page 128

Exam Preparation Triage... There will be many times when you have several tests, papers or other work all due the same week, especially at mid-term. When that happens, do what military doctors and nurses do after a battle when wounded soldiers are lying around bleeding and drying: analyze the situation and save the largest number you can in the shortest period of time by going to those who can be stabilized quickly, then moving to the more needy.

VII
Taking Tests/Exams
Page 156

Most professors like to see an outline. They know the value of outlines. You can score points with a good outline, and it will help you remember everything as well as organize your writing and make it more persuasive. Be as neat with your outline as with your answer itself.

VIII
Papers and Writing
Page 165

The first lesson: DON'T GET STUCK. If you get stuck, get yourself unstuck quick, any way you can. People get stuck because they act like wimps and whine and stare at the wall and feel sorry for themselves. Don't be a big baby. Fire up your brain! Be a man or a woman! Put some words down on paper! Put some clay on the potter's wheel and get going!

The second lesson: An EXCELLENT method of writing is to write your first draft straight from your brain without stopping to look at your sources. Just write what you know and keep moving as fast as possible. The writing is so much more natural and comes easier than when you refer back, constantly, to books, articles and notes.

IX
Presentations
Page 216

"A lawyer friend of mine – a great guy, a very smart guy – came up to me the other day and said he heard that I had spoken in front of 62,000 people in Los Angeles. He said, 'How do you do that? Don't you get scared?' I said, 'I don't want to think about it.' It is true: I don't want to think about it. I just do it. Then he called me up the next day and said, 'That's the smartest thing I've ever heard.'"—Donald Trump

X
Continue Strong
Winning, and the Philosophy of Success
Page 234

"Winning is not everything. It is the only thing."
– Vince Lombardi

"Whether you believe you can do a thing or believe you can't, you are right." – Henry Ford

"The longer I live, the more deeply I am convinced that that which makes the difference between one man and another – between the weak and the powerful, the great and the insignificant – is energy, invincible determination, a purpose once formed and then death or victory."
– Fowell Buxton

"Success or failure in business is caused more by mental attitude even than by mental capacities."
– Walter Dill Scott

"You can really have everything you want. If you go after it. But you will have to want it. The desire for success must be so strong within you that it is the very breath of your life — your first thought when you awaken in the morning, your last thought when you go to bed at night."
– Charles E. Popplestone

"The starting point of all achievement is desire. Keep this constantly in mind. Weak desires bring weak results, just as a small amount of fire makes a small amount of heat." – Napoleon Hill

"People do not lack strength; they lack will."
– Victor Hugo

"Success isn't a result of spontaneous combustion. You must set yourself on fire."
– Arnold H. Glasow

"It's not the size of the man in the fight, it's the size of the fight in the man." – Teddy Roosevelt

Samples from book

240. Forget "easy." Choose topics that you are dying to learn about. You'll be motivated and enjoy it more.

Don't pick paper topics just because you think they are easy, or because a lot of information is available. You will still have to work hard to write the paper, cite your sources and make a persuasive argument. Why do all that with a subject you don't care about?

Pick something you have a passion for, that you are in a white heat to research and learn about. You'll be highly motivated the whole time. Your mind will work so much better.

259. Southern history as it is taught today is a "cultural and political atrocity," and students are being CHEATED.

Esteemed historian, Eugene D. Genovese, who passed away September 26, 2012, was disgusted with the way Southern history is taught today. He writes:

> To speak positively about any part of this Southern tradition is to invite charges of being a racist and an apologist for slavery and segregation. **We are witnessing a cultural and political atrocity** — an increasingly successful campaign by the media and an academic elite to strip young white Southerners, and arguably black Southerners as well, of their heritage, and therefore, their identity. . . .

Two DVD Set

You will RAVE about this talk!

Other Books from
Charleston Athenaeum Press

Professor Edward C. Smith is one of the fore-
most authorities in America on black Confederate soldiers and the participation of blacks on
the Southern side in the War Between the
States. He taught for forty-five years at American
University and was founder and co-director of
the American University Civil War Institute.

He was also a lecturer at the Library of Congress, the Smithsonian Institution, the National
Geographic Society, the National Park Service
and the Historical Society of Washington, D.C.

In this Two-DVD talk that totals over 70 minutes, Professor Smith speaks to an enthusiastic
crowd of the Sons of Confederate Veterans at
their national convention August 12, 1993 in
Lexington, Kentucky.

Not only is Professor Smith fascinating and
articulate, he is witty and broke the crowd up
continuously with laughter and applause. He
received a THUNDEROUS standing ovation at
the end.

There is a ten minute YouTube video clip on:
www.CharlestonAthenaeumPress.com

ISBN: 978-0-9818980-9-4

Note: The drawing of the two black Confederate pickets on the DVD label comes from *Harper's Weekly* January 10, 1863 with caption "Rebel Negro Pickets as Seen Through a Field Glass."

Fiction Set in Charleston, SC!

A Fabulous Kindle Ebook with 31 mostly color IMAGES of Charleston where fights, war, murder and love took place, for $2.99.

ISBN: 978-0-9853632-0-8

- There are six exciting stories in this Kindle ebook.

- 31 IMAGES, mostly full-color photographs of beautiful Charleston, South Carolina.

- Each photograph relates to action in a story, and the story's setting, thus greatly enhancing each story.

- Each gorgeous photograph has a detailed caption with MUCH additional information. Pick up a good bit of Charleston history without even realizing it!

ISBN: 978-0-9853632-0-8 *(ebook)*

Go to Amazon.com and search for:
Charleston SC Short Stories

Index

Finis

Printed in the USA
CPSIA information can be obtained
at www.ICGtesting.com
LVHW041700091123
763115LV00079B/49